We Are the Evidence

We Are the Evidence

A HANDBOOK FOR FINDING YOUR WAY
AFTER SEXUAL ASSAULT

CHEYENNE WILSON

balance

NEW YORK   BOSTON

Balance
Hachette Book Group
1290 Avenue of the Americas
New York, NY 10104
GCP-Balance.com
@GCPBalance

First Edition: June 2024

Balance is an imprint of Grand Central Publishing. The Balance name and logo are registered trademarks of Hachette Book Group, Inc.

The publisher is not responsible for websites (or their content) that are not owned by the publisher.

Balance books may be purchased in bulk for business, educational, or promotional use. For information, please contact your local bookseller or the Hachette Book Group Special Markets Department at special.markets@hbgusa.com.

Library of Congress Control Number: 2024931603

ISBNs: 978-1-5387-4339-3 (trade paperback), 978-1-5387-4340-9 (ebook)

Printed in the United States of America

LSC-C

Printing 1, 2024

To all who have experienced sexual violence and whose strength continues to inspire us all, I hope that this book can shed some light in a time of darkness.

To those who have shared their stories and to those who haven't found their voices yet, I hope this book can spark conversations that allow you to feel safe and know your voice matters.

To a world that needs to change, I dream that this book can act as a catalyst for awareness, empathy, and transformation.

Contents

Part II

Part III

Foreword

Every sixty-eight seconds someone in the United States is sexually assaulted. This breaks down to approximately one in six women and one in thirty-three men (these statistics are from RAINN).

These statistics represent a group that no one should ever have to be a part of, and despite how prevalent sexual assault is, it is still an offense that's not discussed openly and one that leaves victim survivors often feeling isolated and alone with no idea of what they should do in the aftermath or what resources are even available.

Should I report? Will I be believed? Should I get a medical examination? If I get a medical examination, are the police called? Who can I talk to? What can my school or job do? How long do I have to make these decisions? are just some of the questions victim survivors have in the immediate aftermath of a sexual assault.

As sexual assault prosecutors, we have witnessed firsthand the struggles survivors face when trying to answer these questions and navigate the criminal justice system alone. Without clear guidance victim survivors are often left in a gray area, searching from one website to another, finding conflicting information and ending up more confused or disillusioned about what they find. The criminal justice system is difficult, and survivors should never feel alone or like they don't understand the process.

In *We Are the Evidence*, Cheyenne Wilson provides a one-stop resource for survivors; it's a handbook that lets survivors know that they're not alone, that there is a legion of warrior survivors who have walked these horrible steps before them and can help shine a light on the options and answer many questions. Not only is this handbook an important resource, it also arms survivors with information and resources that can help them through this arduous process. Not everyone has a support system, and the criminal justice system is not always survivor-centered, but this handbook will help countless survivors feel less alone through the process.

No one should have to experience a sexual assault, but if the worst has happened to you or a loved one, this handbook can help in answering questions, giving guidance and providing resources so survivors can make the decisions that are the best for them. As sexual assault prosecutors, it's a guide we will recommend to survivors moving forward.

—*Kathryn Marsh, Esq., and Melissa Hoppmeyer, Esq.*

Introduction

I never thought I'd be sexually assaulted, and due to the limited information I had about the realities of sexual assault and commonly held myths, I figured that as long as I avoided the situations and places where rapists were known to lurk, I'd be safe. So, I did the "right" things. I avoided drinking around strangers, wore conservative clothes, and steered clear of dark alleys. When a friendly college classmate invited me over to watch a movie, the idea that I might be harmed didn't even occur to me. At that time, I had no idea that rapists could be friendly classmates who were also obsessed with Disney. But guess what? Sometimes they are.

After I was assaulted, I tried to find information and other resources that would help me to make sense of the confusion I felt and all the questions I had. It was alarming to see how few resources there were, and unbelievable that there wasn't a single comprehensive book that covered what to do after an assault, how to disclose the trauma, how to decide whether to report the crime or seek an alternative form of justice, or how to begin the healing journey.

After two years of confusion, anxiety, and unanswered questions, I stumbled upon an online document for law students about "rape myths." I'd never heard of a rape myth. The document said that more than 80 percent of sexual assaults are committed by people the victims know.

By the time I finished reading that paper, I was angry. Why hadn't I heard the truth about these myths before? Why wasn't there anything like this in the college library when I was searching for answers? If one in six women and one in thirty-three men are likely to be sexually assaulted in their lifetime, why isn't the truth about rape myths being widely publicized? As angry as I was, though, I also felt validated. Finally, I was learning something useful that could help me to move forward with truth and greater clarity. Armed with solid information, I felt empowered to report my sexual assault, face the trial process, and reach out for help to start my healing journey. That's when I realized how powerful information can be for survivors, and that's when I knew I had to write this book. I want to use my trauma, this dark piece of my life story, to light the way for the many others who have been, and will be, victims of sexual violence.

The survivor community is so incredibly beautiful in how we work together to advocate and create resources. I'd had the vision and desire to write this book for years, but I couldn't have done it without the support I've received from others who have experienced this trauma. The emails, Instagram posts, and messages from brave people from around the world kept me going during the times when it would have been a lot easier to give up. The survivors who participated in interviews for this book continually inspired me and reminded me how much everyone in this community wants to help one another.

The number of people experiencing sexual assault grows every hour, and those of us who are already in that group are quick to welcome the new members to a community that none of us want to belong to. We want to take the darkest part of our history and make a positive difference with it. From my own journey and connecting with thousands of other survivors, I'm convinced that knowledge empowers people, and I hope that this accessible and practical handbook will empower more survivors to share their stories, make informed decisions about reporting their assaults, and embark on their healing journeys. I also hope this book encourages people who are not sexual assault survivors to join their voices with ours to advocate for change. The more informed our society is about the realities of sexual assault, the more power we'll have to address this public health crisis. The more power we have, the better we'll be able to make effective changes in our laws, our justice and health care systems, and in the safety and quality of our own lives.

This book was written from one survivor to another. While I'm not a lawyer, doctor, therapist, or law enforcement agent, experts from those fields and others have graciously contributed to this book to provide you with information on topics that are not my areas of experience or expertise. But even with the expert contributions, this book cannot act as a substitute for professional support, treatment, or legal advice. My hope is that you're able to use this information to advocate for yourself and create a plan to move forward. Language has a large impact. Throughout this book, you will see the terms "survivor," "victim," "victim survivor," and "person who was sexually assaulted" used. Everyone will best identify or have different perceptions of each term. Feel free to replace the terms with the words you prefer. This is an individual journey that we're on together, so as you read the suggestions that the experts and other survivors share, you get to decide what you want to include in your journey and how you want to include it. .

Part I

CHAPTER 1

The Truth About Sexual Assault

"What just happened?"

"Did I do anything to suggest I wanted this?"

"Did I say no? If I didn't, does that imply I said yes?"

"If they love me, then it can't be rape, can it?"

"What did I do wrong?"

"What should I do now?"

If you think you may have been sexually assaulted and you're asking questions like these, you're not alone. Many assault survivors are confused about what they experienced and don't know where to look for support or resources. Consider the following examples. Kate didn't seek help after a classmate assaulted her because she knew him, so she thought it didn't count as sexual assault. Now that Benji is a teenager, he knows what his babysitter did was abuse, but it happened so long ago that he doesn't know what to do about it. Lisa's husband comes home drunk and demands sex, and when she says no, he threatens her until she agrees. I didn't know what happened to me was sexual assault until I came across a definition and a list of sexual assault myths—two years after it happened. There are so many of these myths and misconceptions about sexual assault, people aren't initially sure if that's what happened to them. So, let's begin with some important definitions, followed by the biggest myths.

DEFINING SEXUAL ASSAULT

Getting one's mind around sexual assault is difficult enough, but it's an important aspect of the process. First, there are two sets of definitions to be familiar with: legal definitions, which are established in each state, and common definitions, which are used by professionals, experts, advocates, and other sexual assault survivors. It's helpful to know both.

Sexual Assault—Legal Definitions

"Any nonconsensual sexual act proscribed by Federal, tribal, or State law, including when the victim lacks capacity to consent."

—US Department of Justice[1]

"Penetration, no matter how slight, of the vagina or anus with any body part or object, or oral penetration by a sex organ of another person, without the consent of the victim."

—The US Federal Bureau of Investigation[2]

The legal definitions vary from state to state and can be confusing. Fortunately, many states are now adopting the definitions that experts and advocacy resources use. To see how your state defines acts of sexual violence, check out this resource on RAINN.org: https://www.rainn .org/types-sexual-violence.

Most Commonly Used Definitions

These are the definitions that are used throughout the book and in conversations around sexual violence.

Sexual harassment takes place in a workplace or educational setting. It can be directed at a specific person, but it doesn't have to be. Making comments to a coworker about wanting to engage sexually with them can be sexual harassment *and* sending sexual memes to all coworkers can also be a form of sexual harassment. Other examples of sexual harassment can include but are not limited to:

- requesting sexual favors,
- physical or verbal sexual advances,
- someone exposing themselves,
- nonconsensual explicit messages and photos,
- jokes that are sexual in nature,
- having to perform sexual acts to maintain employment or earn promotions.

Sexual assault is sexual contact that is not wanted or explicitly consensual. This includes but is not limited to:

- being coerced or forced to perform sexual acts that you don't want to perform,
- being grabbed, touched, or fondled without your consent,
- attempted rape,
- rape.

Rape is nonconsensual penetration with objects, a penis, or other body parts, including fingers and toes (called digital rape). Not all sexual assault is rape, but all rape is sexual assault.

Other Sexual Assault Terms

Date rape, also called acquaintance rape, is when someone the victim knows forces or coerces them into unwanted sexual acts, typically while on a date. As with all rape, this can be through violence, use of intoxicating substances (including alcohol), peer pressure, threats, or abuse of power.

Intimate partner sexual violence involves sexual assault by a current or former romantic or sexual partner.

THE EVOLUTION OF THE DEFINITION OF RAPE

Definitions of sexual assault and rape are ever-changing, which is one of the many reasons myths about sexual assault continue to exist. In 1927, the Uniform Crime Report (UCR) defined rape as "the carnal knowledge of a female, forcibly, and against her will."[3] This narrow definition included only female victims, because carnal knowledge refers only to penile intercourse with a vagina. By this definition, men and boys couldn't be raped, and it wasn't rape if an object or body part other than the penis is used for penetration.

As reported by the UCR, in 2012, the FBI finally expanded the definition of rape to "penetration, no matter how slight, of the vagina or anus with any body part or object, or oral penetration by a sex organ of another person, without the consent of the victim."[4] This language adjustment, eighty-five years after the previous definition was adopted, was a monumental change for sexual assault survivors.

LET'S TALK ABOUT CONSENT

Consent is more about the presence of a "yes" rather than the absence of a "no." Predators will use the absence of a "no" to justify their predatory behavior. The most commonly used definition of consent is an informed agreement between all participants to partake in a sexual activity.

Abbreviated as FRIES, these are the criteria for a sexual encounter to be consensual:

- **F**reely given—There is no coercion, threat, or power difference that would make you feel that you must say "yes."
- **R**eversible—Consent can be revoked at any time.
- **I**nformed—There is no deception. (For example, if someone says they'll use a condom, but doesn't.)
- **E**nthusiastic—All people involved *want* to be involved.
- **S**pecific—Saying yes to one intimate act doesn't mean you agree to all intimate acts.[5]

Consent is not:

- The absence of "no." If the answer is not an enthusiastic, freely given, informed "yes," it's not a consensual encounter.
- Implied, no matter what someone is wearing, whether they have been drinking, whether they were flirting, or even if they have had consensual sexual encounters with the person in the past. Agreeing to go to someone's home or to a party where there is drinking and dancing doesn't mean or imply that you want to have sex with them.

- Physical signs of arousal. Arousal is a physiological reaction the body has when exposed to certain stimuli. Just like laughing when tickled does not mean that you enjoy being tickled, having a physical response to sexual stimuli does not mean you consent or enjoy what's happening.
- The result of unequal power dynamics.
- A sexual encounter that involves underage participants with adults.
- A sexual encounter that involves participants who are intoxicated, incapacitated, asleep, or unconscious.
- An agreement that is given while a participant is under duress or being intimidated or threatened.

EXPERT CONTRIBUTION:
ALCOHOL-FACILITATED SEXUAL ASSAULT
Retired Detective Justin Boardman, of Boardman Training and Consulting

Alcohol-facilitated sexual assault refers to incidents in which alcohol consumption is used as a tool to exploit and incapacitate victims, leaving them vulnerable to sexual violence. It's a pervasive issue that demands a sensitive response by law enforcement and the justice system. The importance of empathy, being trauma-informed, and providing necessary resources is paramount. Victims can face unique challenges, and law enforcement can play a crucial role in their recovery.

Offenders use alcohol to manipulate and groom to obtain control and exploit victims for personal gain. By understanding the dynamics of manipulation and grooming, you may be able to understand that what happened to you was not your fault. It was a calculated and deliberate act by the person who assaulted you. Offenders use these deceptive tactics and alcohol to influence or control others. It often involves exploiting vulnerabilities, distorting information, and using emotional manipulation to gain power over someone. Some common signs of manipulation besides alcohol can include excessive flattery, gaslighting, isolation from friends and family, and the use of guilt or fear to control the victim.

Alcohol first affects one's mental status, then starts affecting motor skills. It is used to reduce victims' inhibitions and relax their boundaries. It will also make the offender's actions of manipulation less noticeable as the alcohol intoxication continues, affecting the victim's ability to resist along with the trauma of the event.

Alcohol can affect the offender by lowering inhibitions and giving them the confidence to make the move to victimize.

The justice system should provide a safe and non-judgmental environment, conduct thorough medical examinations, offer psychological support, and collaborate with law enforcement agencies. One of the first steps in the response to a victim of alcohol-facilitated sexual assault is to establish a safe and non-judgmental environment. By doing so, the justice system can help alleviate the shame and self-blame often experienced. Victims often experience a range of emotional and psychological distress, including post-traumatic stress disorder (PTSD), anxiety, depression, and feelings of guilt or shame.

The shame experienced by victims of sexual assault often stems from societal attitudes and misconceptions surrounding sexual violence. These same attitudes can also affect law enforcement and the justice system. This response can lead victims to internalize feelings of shame, believing that they are somehow at fault for the assault. You are not at fault.

COMMON TYPES OF MANIPULATION

Sexual assault is confusing to navigate for most survivors, and layers of manipulation, gaslighting, or grooming can make it even more confusing and also lead to self-blame. Perpetrators of sexual violence can use tools like manipulation, grooming, or gaslighting as a way to identify, isolate, and abuse survivors.

Grooming: When someone builds a relationship or connection with a child or adult with the intention to sexually exploit or abuse them. Grooming can start online or in person, but the first step is for the perpetrator to gain the intended victim's trust.

Grooming can include but is not limited to:

- targeting someone, finding out what their vulnerabilities are, and gaining their trust,
- isolating someone and finding ways to be alone with them,
- a lot of touching, which often starts with non-sexual touching.

Coercion: When someone persuades you to do something through manipulation or threats. An offender may use their body, their words, or their tone to threaten and intimidate the intended victim. The following are common examples of coercive statements:

- "I thought you loved me?"
- "I have waited months. How much longer should I be patient?"
- "You've done it with other people, so what's the big deal?"
- "Sex is a coping mechanism for me; don't you want to help me?"
- "If you don't want to have sex with me, it must mean that you are getting your needs met elsewhere."
- "Your job might be in jeopardy if you don't."

- "But I'm your boyfriend/girlfriend and I have waited long enough for you."
- "Just relax and do it."
- "I have been with sexual assault victims before, and they all were okay having sex."
- "I won't put it in, I just want to rub you with it."
- "I'm going to marry you eventually, so it really doesn't matter."
- "I know you want to. If you didn't, why would you make me feel like this?"
- "Don't you trust me?"
- "You owe me."
- "Come on, it will help me feel better."
- "If you don't know why you are saying no, shouldn't it be a yes?"
- "I will hurt myself if you don't do it."

Gaslighting: When someone manipulates another person to make them question their reality. Abusers and perpetrators may use this tactic to make their victims question or doubt their own knowledge of what occurred. Examples of a rapist gaslighting their victim may look like:

- "You don't remember? You said you wanted it at the time."
- "I would never do that to you. You're remembering it wrong."
- "If you think I'm some kind of rapist, why are you even talking to me?"

These types of statements can be incredibly confusing for someone who has been assaulted. If it makes them doubt if what happened was sexual assault, they may feel like other people won't believe them and be less likely to reach out for help.

EXPERT CONTRIBUTION: SIGNS OF SEXUAL ABUSE IN CHILDREN AND HOW TO OFFER SUPPORT
Amanda Schonhardt, BSW

Knowing the signs of sexual abuse in children and how to communicate with them about it is essential because children don't always know that what's happening is inappropriate, and they may not know how to talk about it.

Signs or behaviors that could indicate a child is being sexually abused include:

- excessive talk about sexual topics abnormal for the child's age/development,
- inappropriate knowledge of sexual behavior/actions for their age,
- onset of anxiety or fear of being around a specific individual,
- decrease in confidence or self-image (suddenly wearing oversized clothing, dressing down, etc.),
- decrease in hygiene (e.g., not showering),
- medical issues such as STDs,
- self-harm,
- suddenly has gifts, money, new toys, etc. (seen in trafficking/manipulation),
- children regressing to toddler behaviors such as sucking thumbs, bed-wetting, etc.

How to talk to kids or teens about sexual abuse and be a safe person for them:

Use proper terminology when teaching your children about body parts. Using nicknames will make it hard for adults or others to

understand if they are talking about being touched somewhere inap-
propriately. When talking or asking children about touches, don't label
them as good and bad touches. Rather, explore them as touches they
may like or not like. Often victims of child abuse don't realize the
touches they are receiving are bad; they are often coached and told these
things are okay if they're done by someone they trust or love. Don't
shame a child if they state they liked the touch or the feelings that they
had with the touches. They don't know that they shouldn't be touched
this way, and just like adults they may be aroused by this and may not
know this isn't supposed to be occurring. Parents need to be aware and
educated on internet trafficking and soliciting of children. Also make
sure you're knowledgeable about safety features for phones and tablets.
Learn how to control chat features, location sharing, and video settings
in your child's devices. Have conversations with your child about their
private body parts and who should and should not be touching them,
seeing them, and/or asking about them. Educate children that their body
belongs to them, and it's okay to say no to someone wanting to see or
touch them. Within this, it is also important for children to know they
can talk to doctors, teachers, and other professionals if they don't feel
safe talking to their parents.

When talking with a child about concerns of sex abuse, don't put
words into their mouth. Say things like, "Tell me about what worries
you about..." and "Tell me more about that" instead of using direct
questions.

Teach your child it's okay to say no to anything that makes them
feel unsafe or uncertain. Assure them that they won't be in trouble for
taking charge of their own emotions and feelings for their body, that
their body belongs to them, and it's okay for them to take ownership
of that.

Educate children that no one should want to or have reason to show them their private parts, and if someone tells them that this is okay, they need to tell a trusted adult.

Normalize conversations about the body at a young age by talking about private body parts and about who is and is not able to help take care of their body.

12 MYTHS ABOUT SEXUAL ASSAULT

Sexual assault myths are damaging beliefs, often based on stereotypes, that are typically used to excuse sexually violent behavior or shift the blame from the perpetrator to the victim. These dangerous myths, which are perpetuated by ignorance, the judicial system, the legal system, and the media, have become ingrained in our culture. These myths can:

- Make us repeatedly question if we somehow share the blame for the crime.
- Make us question whether what happened is a valid crime that's worth reporting.
- Make it harder for people to believe our accounts of what happened.
- Make it harder for us to receive support.
- Prevent jurors from feeling confident about delivering a guilty verdict.

We need to dispel these myths because they protect perpetrators. People who believe the myths tend to doubt the survivors who disclose this crime, instead of being supportive listeners. Also, importantly, jurors need to be more informed for court proceedings. Dispelling myths will help them to identify and see through defendants' excuses— which are often based on widely accepted myths.

Myth #1: You can only be assaulted by strangers.

"I knew I hadn't consented, but I knew him and I trusted him, so I thought it couldn't be rape. Weren't rapists strangers or stalkers? Since I didn't think it was rape, I blamed myself and thought I couldn't report it."

According to the Department of Justice, between 80 and 94 percent of sexual assaults are committed by someone the victim knows.[6] Current and former spouses and partners commit 33 percent of assaults.

When the victim is a minor, 93 percent know their perpetrator and 34 percent of perpetrators are family members.[7]

DID YOU KNOW YOUR ABUSER OR RAPIST?

Two hundred followers of the We are the Evidence platform who were sexually assaulted responded to the question, "Did you know your perpetrator?" Only one survivor said no. The following are an assortment of the responses we received.

"He was my uncle."

"She was a 'friend' of my mother."

"We had recently met. I accepted a date invitation and was raped during our date."

"I barely knew him. He was a professor in the same department where I was getting my doctorate, and we matched on Bumble."

"He was a trusted friend. We met when I was twelve and he was twenty-eight."

"My father."

"He was a coworker of mine at a resort."

"They were one of my closest friends at the time."

"He was my boyfriend of five years."

"It was my grandfather and stepfather."

"I was raped by a client."

"He was an ex-boyfriend. At the time of the assault, we had broken up but remained good friends."

"My mother."

"College classmate."

"Friend of a friend."

"My cousin."

"He was someone who approached me in a bar."

"My first boyfriend."

"My ex-girlfriend."

"My teammate's brother."

"Someone I had previously been in a long-term relationship with."

"My best friend's boyfriend."

"I was married to him."

"My brother."

"He was my mother's best friend. He watched me grow up."

"Boyfriend that I met at church."

"Leader in the military who worked in the cafeteria while I was overseas."

"My dad, then his colleague."

"He was an LPN at the senior living facility I volunteered at."

"He was a senior math teacher at my school."

"He was the swim coach at the local pool I went to."

"He is the son of my parents' friend. We grew up together."

"We were in the same workout program."

"I was sold to him for my friend to get drug money."

"My brother-in-law."

"Mine was my sister's forty-five-year-old boyfriend."

"My adoptive father."

"Male babysitter."

"Female babysitter."

"Random men my father would bring home to 'pay' for me."

"One was my uncle, and then I was adopted, and it was my adoptive brother."

"My dance teacher growing up."

> "Mine was a family friend, one of the older neighborhood kids that used to live down the road from me."
>
> "Mom's new live-in boyfriend, later became my stepfather."
> "Deacon in our church."

Myth #2: You could have stopped the assault by resisting harder.

"My entire life I had believed that if I was being sexually violated and assaulted that I would fight back. I had heard and believed that if I put up a fight the person would be more likely to stop. I was so confused about why I didn't fight, it made me question if it could be assault, since I didn't resist. Why didn't I fight back?"

There are many reasons you might not have fought back against your perpetrator. Your brain will try to protect you at all costs, which is where the trauma responses can come into play—we'll spend more time on those in chapter four. Choosing not to resist could have been your body's way of trying to prevent the assault from escalating. There are also instances when someone resists, but they're physically overpowered, and a different trauma response takes over, such as the freeze response. The reality is that no one knows how they'll respond in a traumatic situation until they're in it. Ultimately, someone else took advantage of you and harmed you. That wasn't your decision. They're to blame, not you.

Myth #3: Rapists are easy to spot.

"None of us knew her; she was a stranger to me. But I never considered her to be a threat or to be someone who would harm me. My trust made me vulnerable."

While it might be comforting to believe that nobody we know has committed a violent crime and that we'd be able to spot a rapist if we saw one, both beliefs create a false sense of security. They also make it harder for people who are uninformed or misinformed to believe that victims have been assaulted.

Myth #4: You did something to deserve being assaulted.

"I agreed to go to his house. For the longest time I blamed myself, when all I ever consented to was going to his house."

You didn't ask to be assaulted, and you definitely didn't do anything to deserve it. But because this myth is so prevalent, many survivors assume some of the blame. If you're feeling responsible for what happened because you agreed to go on a date with someone, or because of what you were wearing, how you were dancing, or anything else that wasn't explicit consent, know that it wasn't your fault; that going on a date, wearing an item of clothing, or anything else does not mean you deserved what happened to you.

Myth #5: Women want to be raped.

"I begged him to stop, and he just kept saying he knew I wanted to be a 'bad girl.' That I was only saying no to look like I was being good when he knew better. He said he knew I really wanted this. I will never forget how meaningless my 'no' was."

Regardless of what you've heard, read, or seen in films, women do not want to be raped. If you did not freely and enthusiastically say "yes," it's sexual assault.

Myth #6: Men can't be sexually assaulted.

"My own family member, who was a doctor, didn't believe me when I said I was assaulted. They didn't understand apparently how I could have let that happen. I didn't tell anyone else again until years later I was admitted to inpatient for

self-harm and someone finally told me that men could in fact be assaulted. I wasn't weak. It wasn't my fault. I am not the only one."

There is very little data about the prevalence of men being sexually assaulted, and numbers that have previously been published are probably inaccurate because in many cases male victims face even more barriers to reporting than female victims. Many men in the We Are the Evidence community have reported that people didn't believe them when they disclosed their assault. Instead of support, they've heard comments like, "How could that even work?" or "You weren't strong enough to stop her?" and "That couldn't have happened if you didn't have an erection, so you must have liked it." An erection is not consent (see Sexual Assault Myth #8); everyone experiences different trauma responses, and everyone deserves to have support and resources available to them.

Myth #7: Only virgins can be raped.

"I was raised to believe that it was my duty to please my husband. Whether or not I wanted to have sex with him didn't matter. After I had lost my virginity to him, I lost the right to refuse him, and whenever I tried to refuse him, he would force me."

Your previous sexual experiences do not indicate consent for future sexual encounters, even if you've had sex with that person before. You have the right to say no to anyone, at any time.

Myth #8: It isn't rape if you have an erection or an orgasm.

"When it was happening, she would comment on my body's reaction and say that was proof I wanted it. I didn't want it. I don't know how to explain that to other guys, though."

Arousal and orgasms are complex biological reactions that we do not control, so physical signs of arousal and biological reactions to a stimulus are not consent. Without having this understanding, a survivor's shame and guilt can stop them from seeking support and reporting.

Myth #9: Survivors of assault will act hysterical.

"During the closing statements of my trial, the defense attorney stood in front of the jury and pointed out that I didn't cry when I was on the stand. They asked the jury if someone could really be traumatized if they didn't cry when recounting the events of their assault. I still blame myself for the not guilty verdict. If I had cried, would they have believed me?"

The myth that victims will or should respond a certain way after they're assaulted is extraordinarily harmful. People tend to respond to trauma and high-stress situations (such as testifying in court) in at least five different ways: fight, flight, freeze, fawn, and flop. We cover these in more detail in chapter four.

Myth #10: It isn't rape if a weapon wasn't involved.

"I didn't think anyone would believe me. It's not like I was held at gunpoint or anything. I could have probably overpowered them or screamed, and I didn't do either. I just froze."

According to a survey conducted by the Department of Justice in 2013, only 11 percent of rapes and sexual assaults involved a weapon.[8] Date rape drugs and alcohol can also be used to incapacitate someone or to make it easy to restrain a victim before an assault.

Myth #11: If it was really sexual assault, you would have reported it right away.

"People keep asking me why I didn't report if it was really assault. To be honest it didn't seem worth it. I didn't know what to do, I didn't know who to

trust, and I wasn't sure that I wanted to ruin my offender's life. I just wanted to move on."

Choosing not to report or waiting to report does not minimize the crime. There are many reasons why people don't report sexual assault right away, or at all. Many survivors aren't sure if what they experienced was assault and also know that getting a conviction is an uphill battle. According to the Department of Justice in its National Crime Victimization Survey, out of 1,000 sexual assaults, 310 will be reported to law enforcement and only 25 perpetrators will be incarcerated.[9] So it's no wonder that reporting can look hopeless.

There are other reasons why a victim may choose not to report:

- They fear retaliation.
- They did not think they would be believed or would receive help from law enforcement.
- They worried about, or weren't sure, if they wanted to get the perpetrator in legal trouble.
- They didn't want to relive the assault through the reporting process.
- They were told by friends and family not to report.

Myth #12: If it had been sexual assault, there would be physical evidence.

"They asked me where the evidence was that I had been assaulted. But what evidence were they possibly needing or hoping to find? My rapist was my significant other; any evidence that they might have even found I knew that my rapist would just say it was consensual anyways."

Asking a survivor to use physical evidence to prove they were sexually assaulted is often unrealistic. Consider the following variables:

- Survivors often know the perpetrator and have interacted with them before the assault, so their DNA can often be found on each other for reasons other than sexual assault.
- Survivors don't collect evidence if they don't initially know that it was sexual assault.

Even if a survivor is physically injured, there may not be evidence of the injuries by the time they have an exam or report the crime.

EXPERT CONTRIBUTION: THE POWER OF WORDS
Patricia Bathory, MBA, MACP, CCC

Words have power, and they have different subjective meaning to different people. When talking about sexual assault, some individuals who have gone through it refuse to use the word "victim," preferring "survivor." They believe that all of their work and their healing journey has made them a survivor, and the word "victim" feels disempowering. This is extremely valid and true for many survivors.

Other individuals are not ready to let go of the word "victim" because they feel that this is the best word that describes what happened to them. They are not ready to let go of the idea that a crime was committed against them, and that fundamentally makes them a victim. For these individuals, being a victim of a crime is not the same as having a victim mentality. As one of my clients says, "The fact that I didn't let my rape define me, and the fact that I worked really hard to heal and move forward, does not take away the fact that I was a victim of a crime perpetrated against me." She feels the word "survivor" to be too positive, denying the effect the rape has every day of her life.

No one term is more correct than the other—it's what you find more empowering that you should use.

Isabella's Story

I was five years old the first time I was abused, and like so many other survivors, it was by someone I knew and trusted. Little did I know then, that was just the beginning. Throughout my childhood, I was abused by seven different people—all of them known by me or my parents.

As a child, I didn't know what was happening. Deep inside I knew something felt wrong, but I didn't have the awareness or understanding to process the trauma. And sadly, after being assaulted by several people, body violations began to feel like a part of my life. I didn't know what it felt like to have ownership over my body, nor could I begin to understand what it would mean long-term for people to recurrently assert physical and emotional control over me. At the end of the day, children translate their experiences into inner feelings of safety, and all I knew and understood was that I was not safe. Without a secure and trusting foundation, my childhood felt chaotic. I didn't feel stable at home or at school.

Looking back now, I realize the only time I ever felt like myself was in dance class.

I started dancing before I could walk. My parents joke that I was creating and directing dance shows with my brother (definitely not a dancer, but always a good sport) before I could fully talk. As a child, I was in dance class five days a week. And it was there where I felt like a more free and complete version of myself. It was a physical and emotional release—I was able to connect with my body, and I had a safe and supportive outlet to let go of whatever my body was storing. This feeling starkly contrasted with those periods when dance wasn't affordable, like during high school after my parents' separation. During those times, I was more isolated and confused. My body didn't feel like mine, and I experienced almost full-time active dissociation, which led me as a teenager to try to take my life twice.

The only thing that seemed to bring the light back in after those dark times was getting back into dance. Dance let me rediscover the feelings of peace and true comfort. Although I might not have been able to fully understand it until years later, I learned a big truth quite young—dance was never going to be just a hobby for me. It was always going to be an emotional, physical, and spiritual practice. Dance class was my home, at times my only safe home, and it helped me feel more like myself. Moving my body actually helps me process and release the trauma of my abuse. In that way, I think dance was not only my first love, but my first healer, too.

After doing some inner work, I knew I wanted to share the healing effects of dance with others. In 2014, I founded She-Is, a 501(c)3 nonprofit based in Los Angeles that teaches dance to survivors of sexual abuse and sex trafficking. Since 2014, we've taught dance to more than 1,000 survivors in the US and internationally. We visit countries in southeast Asia annually to hold two-week survivor workshops with young girls who have been rescued from the sex trade.

As we've worked with these survivors over the years, I've seen that my own story may differ in specifics from other survivors, but the impact of dance and movement therapy is the same for all of us. Every survivor can benefit from reclaiming their body ownership and building confidence. All of us can benefit from dancing together as a group, because it builds community and a sense of shared understanding across our experiences. This deepens our awareness of others and our ability to process our own experiences through empathy and compassion for others. The awakening of our physical senses helps release stored trauma from the inside out. In this way, therapeutic dance classes become a container for healing and growth. While it's possible to do this work individually, healing in a collective is a revolutionary and powerful tool for those who feel isolated in their trauma and past experiences. It's been an honor and privilege to share space with other survivors in this way.

Today, dance remains one of my favorite healing methods. I've supplemented it with a variety of other healing modalities, including acupuncture, hypnosis, EFT tapping, and talk therapy. This toolkit supports my complexity as a person and survivor on my healing journey, but the accessibility of dance is one reason I recommend it to all trauma survivors. Dancing is one of the most natural things in the world. Most of us sway along to music as babies before we can walk or talk. Music is everywhere, and the only thing we need to dance is our body. By ourselves or with a group, online or in person, in an organized class or freestyling in our bedroom, reconnecting with our body through movement is what matters. It is inclusive of every body type, gender, sexual orientation, experience, skill level, and beyond. Dance is for everyone. So is healing.

For any and all survivors out there, I want you to know you are special and you are loved. You deserve a beautiful life and are worthy of beautiful things. I see you and I believe in you. Please reach out to others for support. There are resources and so many people willing to help. You are worth it.

For those interested in taking a dance class, I recommend checking out local groups, taking online classes, or reaching out to us at She-Is. We host free monthly survivor classes and will be so happy to see you there. We're in this together.

—Isabella Grosso, Founder of She-Is, Los Angeles, California

LET'S CHECK IN

When I first learned what sexual assault is and what consent should involve, I was flooded with confusing thoughts, feelings, and even more questions than I'd had before. I was angry, sad, and scared, but I was also relieved because I finally understood the truth about what I'd experienced. So, here are some questions you can ask yourself to help process the content in this chapter:

- What sexual assault myths have affected your beliefs about your assault and about yourself?
- Is there any blame you continue to hold on to? Are you ready to let that go?
- What's one kind thing you can do for yourself today?

In addition to all the emotions you may be experiencing, I encourage you to leave some space to feel proud of yourself for beginning this healing journey.

CHAPTER 2

What to Do If You've Been Assaulted

It may be that you've come to this book just after your assault, or it may be years or even decades later. No matter where you are on your journey, and before we approach these next steps, know that the entire survivor community is behind you. It is one that none of us wished to join, but we stand together, and we stand with you.

I know there's nothing I can say to take away the pain of your experience, but I hope the information shared here will help you feel a little less afraid and a little less alone. First, there are some things you need to hear:

You are incredibly brave for seeking out this information.
You are so much stronger than anyone should have to be.
You survived the assault, and you will survive your healing journey.
No matter what, you didn't ask for this.
You matter.

EXPERT CONTRIBUTION: THE ROLE OF AN ADVOCATE FOR SURVIVORS OF SEXUAL VIOLENCE

Bree Theising-Stair, Sexual Violence Advocate

The Violence Against Women Act (VAWA)/Victims of Crime Act (VOCA)/Family Violence Prevention and Services Act (FVPSA) is a federal law that states that victim service providers who receive this funding (VAWA, VOCA, and FVPSA) shall not disclose any identifying information of victims/survivors they are working with unless that person consents, there is a statutory requirement to do so, or case law mandates victim service providers to do so.

A sexual assault counselor has undergone the state-mandated forty-plus hours of training to work in a sexual violence agency and is under supervision during their duties. The primary focus of a sexual assault counselor is to provide guidance and assist victims/survivors who have experienced sexual violence in making informed decisions. Sexual assault counselors come from various backgrounds of education and do not provide traditional therapy you would receive with a licensed mental health provider. In turn, we have moved to referring to our trained providers as sexual violence advocates.

Advocates promote or support the interests of a cause or a group. The shift from calling providers sexual assault counselors to sexual violence advocates is because we're trained to help provide information and support for victims/survivors and collaborate with you so you are heard. We do not provide a mental health diagnosis or treatment, but rather support you throughout the journey. We use the term "sexual violence" instead of "sexual assault" as sexual violence encompasses all forms of sexual violence, including, but not limited to, drug-facilitated sexual assault, human trafficking, and incest.

A victim witness advocate is different than a sexual violence advocate. Victim witness advocates do not hold the same confidentiality. This means anything you say to a victim witness advocate is shared with the prosecution, whereas anything shared with a sexual violence advocate is confidential and not shared unless it's a mandated report.

A victim/survivor can request that a sexual violence advocate be present with them throughout their court proceedings. You're not required to be present at all hearings; it is your preference unless there is a subpoena. Typically, if subpoenaed to testify, you will only need to be present at the trial. This may include, but is not limited to, an omnibus hearing, pre-trial, trial, sentencing, and appeals.

While sexual violence advocates come from a variety of educational backgrounds, we all join this work because we see the immense need to advocate for those who may have lost their voice temporarily, and we want to help them get it back. Another attribute we have in common is that we are here to meet the victims/survivors where they are and not define their journey for them.

YOUR NEXT STEPS

Many people who have been sexually assaulted don't immediately realize what they experienced was a trauma, and not knowing can affect the decisions you make and the actions you decide to take after the assault. For now, the most important thing is that you find a way to feel safe so you can decide how you want to move forward. Use this section as it applies to you and your specific situation. If you aren't ready to take action steps yet, that's totally okay.

Make Your Way to the Safest Place Possible

Since everyone's trauma is different, the places and things that give you a sense of safety may be different than the places and things that help other survivors to feel safe. Immediately after being assaulted, try to visit a hospital so you can have an examination and also begin the reporting process if you know you want to report. (See chapter three for more information about sexual assault forensic examinations.) Your safety is of the highest importance, so if you live with or near the person who assaulted you, you work with them, or go to school with them, the first step is to protect yourself, and that often means leaving the unsafe situation or environment. Some places to consider going are the local police station, a place of faith, an advocacy center, a safe person's house, or a public place if you'll feel safer with other people around.

Besides locations, think about what else might help you to feel safer. Is there a personal item that brings you comfort, like a soft blanket or favorite sweater? Will a warm cup of tea help to ground you? Do you have a pet that helps you feel safe?

IF YOU LIVE WITH YOUR ABUSER

If your abuser is someone you live with, you might not feel safe enough to process the abuse or address the abuse until you've found somewhere that's safe for you to go. If you need to leave home, here are some steps to consider:

- If possible, try to start saving money, even if it's just a small amount at a time.
- Share the abuse and concerns with someone you trust so they know to check in on you daily in case things escalate.
- Pack a bag that has the essentials you'll need if you have to leave home quickly. Hide it somewhere in your home, your car, at work, or with a trusted friend or family member. In addition to essentials (clothes, medications, phone), pack important documents like medical records, birth certificates, Social Security cards, and vehicle titles.
- Keep your phone charged at all times.

- Keep your car fueled up and ready to go.
- Make a list of important phone numbers and keep it with you, in addition to storing the numbers in your phone.

Reach Out for Help

Sexual assault survivors often feel isolated, especially when carrying such a burden alone. For most survivors, the first hours and days after the assault are confusing—it's very difficult to process the initial shock of your trauma on your own. For this reason, I suggest you first seek out professional resources. Note that the first professional resource you reach out to may not have all the answers you need, but they can direct you to places that might be more helpful to you, and they can offer validation and support in moments when you don't feel like you can turn to someone you know. Here are some resources you can start with. Information about the role of a sexual violence advocate and the support they can provide you is provided on page 27 by Bree Theising-Stair, advocate for survivors of sexual violence.

Find Support on the Crisis Line

Sexual violence centers depend widely on volunteers to help maintain their 24/7 status as crisis response agencies. Most stand-alone sexual violence centers or dual programs for domestic violence and sexual violence have a 24/7 crisis line. This allows victims/survivors of sexual violence to reach and speak to an advocate any time of day or night. You can ask questions about services, reporting options, medical exam options, and processing of current thoughts and feelings. This is a space for victims/survivors to remain anonymous should they choose to or to openly identify themselves. The crisis line is not a space where victims/survivors have to go through their traumatic experiences verbally in order to be helped. The crisis line and sexual assault advocates do not want to retraumatize callers by having them explain their trauma in detail. Sexual assault advocates are trained to use active listening when responding to crisis.

Get Support During a Forensic Evidence Collection Exam

Sexual violence centers work with medical facilities and sexual assault nurse examiner (SANE) programs on forensic evidence collection. Advocates will be asked to respond and support victims/survivors during their medical exams. This service is provided 24/7 and involves explaining the reporting options, medical exam options, advocacy options, and being there for the victim/survivor. Advocates can also explain what happens in a forensic exam so victims/survivors can make informed decisions about their care.

Continuing Support After Sexual Violence

Sexual violence centers offer one-to-one support advocacy after the sexual assault. One-to-one support advocacy is based on a trauma-informed psychoeducation evidence-based practice. Trauma-informed care is provided by meeting the victim/survivor where you are. There is no curriculum for you to follow in order to process and heal as everyone's journey is individual.

Advocates do not define your trauma nor tell you how and where you should be on your journey. They help you to process the trauma you have experienced up to this point in life. Psychoeducation is provided by advocates to lay out information and offer support with coping, processing, and healing from sexual violence. One-to-one support advocacy may also involve assisting in referrals to other professionals to aid with prominent needs, including housing, emergency financial assistance, and therapy.

Crime victim reparation is available in all states within the United States of America. Sexual assault advocates can assist in filling out the form and submission for this service. There are varying qualifications and degrees of financial reimbursement for victims/survivors from state to state.

EXPERT CONTRIBUTION: BARRIERS TO REPORTING FOR BLACK WOMEN, AND RESOURCES FOR ADDITIONAL SUPPORT
Maggie Wagner, Communications Coordinator at the Legal Action Center in New York

For Black women, navigating the choices after sexual assault can be a far different journey from what white women experience. While all survivors may face sexism in the legal system, for Black women it's compounded by deep-seated racism. And that poses unique challenges when it comes to deciding if and how to report and finding means of healing from the trauma.

Attempts to convince a judge, jury, detective, or doctor that an assault occurred and should be treated as a violent crime are often met with doubt—doubt based in racist misconceptions that Black women are more promiscuous than white women, which contribute to a misguided belief that violence against them is a less serious crime than violence against white women. Beyond these harmful mindsets about Black women, Black communities have been perpetually persecuted and punished by the US criminal legal system at higher rates than white people, resulting in an understandable distrust of that system.

The consequences of these barriers can be seen in the startlingly low reporting rates by Black women survivors. Despite the fact that Black women experience assault at a rate higher than white women do, it's estimated that only one rape out of every sixteen committed against them is reported. Considering that reporting involves interacting with police departments, which have been publicly implicated in numerous deaths of Black people, and court systems, which are incarcerating Black people at nearly five times the rate of white people, it's no surprise that Black women often choose *not* to report.

Another factor that's made the landscape treacherous for Black women is the stigma surrounding mental health conditions. The stigma is often more pronounced in Black communities, where such conditions may be perceived as weaknesses, making it a strong deterrent to seeking therapy and other mental health support. And those who do want to pursue support are faced with the reality that trauma-informed mental health care providers of color are few and far between.

Among the other obstacles Black women face is the fact that they're more likely than white women to exist at the intersection of marginalized communities, such as those facing homelessness and joblessness. All told, Black women are caught in a societal cycle where their human rights to justice and dignity are often out of reach.

Obviously, the criminal legal system is in need of sweeping reform as it relates to the reporting of sexual assault, but until that's achieved, there are resources available for Black women and avenues of advocacy for all of us who want to address the intertwining barriers Black women face. Access to trauma-informed providers is far from equitable, but many national and local organizations are fighting to provide resources targeted to Black survivors, such as directories of therapists of color, mental health and healing services, and free legal services. Examples include:

- Therapy for Black Girls, Inclusive Therapists, Ayana Therapists, and Innopsych, which provide services for finding mental health providers of color.
- Love WITH Accountability, a project focused on ending childhood sexual abuse and adult rape in Black communities. They

provide a list of organizations and collectives led by BIPOC (Black, Indigenous, and people of color) survivors.

- me too. Resource Library, which allows you to search for therapists, shelters, social services, crisis intervention, and more using demographic filters.
- There are also many local organizations that provide healing and legal services. For example, The Safe Sisters Circle, based in Washington, DC, provides both healing and legal services to Black women survivors of domestic violence and sexual assault (202-365-5251). And New York City–based Black Women's Blueprint supports and advocates for Black women survivors of gender-based violence (646-256-1242).

For those interested in making the reporting and healing experiences equitable, advocacy work is key and should be guided by the voices and experiences of Black survivors. Policy changes are needed to address widespread discrimination against Black people, promote access to and availability of trauma-informed providers of color, and explore alternative routes of justice. There are many national organizations engaging in strategies like technical assistance for community-based organizations, policy advocacy, and the providing of health and legal resources to level the field and emphasize healing. Examples include:

- National Black Women's Justice Institute (718-715-0261)
- National Organization of Sisters of Color Ending Sexual Assault
- Black Women's Health Imperative (888-834-8451)
- Ujima (The National Center on Violence Against Women in the Black Community) (1-844-77-UJIMA)
- Black Emotional and Mental Health Collective

Everyone should have the opportunity to report their assault and find means of healing in ways that cater to their individual needs. Black women survivors rarely get this chance. The above resources are an important starting point in ensuring that Black women survivors can define and navigate justice and healing on their terms.

HOTLINES

Even if you've told some people about what happened to you, it can sometimes feel safer to reach out to a hotline or otherwise connect with a platform of survivors. Hotlines became an important part of my healing, though I felt hesitant about calling one the first time. There was a time in my healing process where I felt frequent intrusive suicidal thoughts, and eventually, despite my initial hesitation, I called the National Suicide Hotline. My hesitation came from feeling like I would be a burden to the resource, that my trauma wasn't serious enough to call a hotline, and I didn't even know what I would say. But as soon as I started talking, I could feel myself calming down, just a bit. Over time, I've learned that hotlines are really helpful when you just need to talk to someone who will listen to what you're going through and also to learn about additional resources such as local sexual assault advocacy centers. Hotline staff are trained in a variety of topics such as active listening, crisis intervention, and resource referrals. There are several hotlines you can access, depending on your circumstances, and all of those listed here are free. If you're in the midst of an emergency, don't call a hotline: call 911 for an emergency response.

NATIONAL SEXUAL ASSAULT HOTLINE: 1-800-656-4673

This hotline is available 24/7 to provide free support and connect you and your loved ones to resources that are needed after sexual assault.

National Suicide Hotline: 988 (call or text)

The National Suicide Hotline is open 24/7 with availability via chat and phone call options to provide free support to those who are in crisis, or those who are supporting someone going through a crisis.

National Domestic Violence Hotline: Call 1-800-799-7233 or Text "START" at 88788

The National Domestic Violence Hotline is a free hotline available 24/7 to those experiencing domestic violence or those who have a loved one experiencing domestic violence.

Childhelp National Child Abuse Hotline: 800-422-4453

The National Child Abuse Hotline provides 24/7 free support to help identify abuse and share information about what to do if you suspect there is abuse.

Darkness to Light (for Child Abuse/Sexual Abuse): Call 800-686-HOPE or Text "HOME" to 741741

This hotline provides support and resources for those who have experienced child sexual abuse.

National Human Trafficking Resource Center: Call 888-373-7888 or Text "INFO" to 233733

The National Human Trafficking Resource Center provides services to survivors and witnesses of human trafficking to help connect them to resources.

StrongHearts Native Helpline: 844-762-8483

StrongHearts Native Helpline provides culturally appropriate support to Native Americans who have experienced sexual violence.

The Network/La Red: 617-742-4911 or 800-832-1901

This hotline supports survivors of partner abuse in LGBTQ, polyamorous, and kink communities.

The Trevor Project: Call 866-488-7386 or Text "START" to 678-678

The Trevor Project is an online crisis chat and hotline that supports LGBTQ youth in crisis.

DoD Safe Helpline: 877-995-5247

The DoD Safe Helpline is a crisis support service created for members of the Department of Defense community who have been affected by sexual assault.

Even if you don't think you want or need to call these hotlines, please consider writing down the ones you might want to call later, or save the numbers in your phone. That way, you'll have them if you need them, and you'll be able to share them with friends if they need them. Hotlines do add a level of human connection and emotional support that you might not get from online or paper resources such as a book.

ONLINE RESOURCES

Online resources offer the convenience of providing general guidance on a wide range of topics. You may feel better processing information initially alone before connecting to other people about your trauma.

NATIONAL SEXUAL VIOLENCE RESOURCE CENTER (WWW.NSVRC.ORG)

This website offers a wide range of resources on sexual violence prevention, education, research, and tools to support survivors and organizations that support survivors.

RAINN (RAINN.ORG)

RAINN offers support services and resources for sexual assault survivors, including hotline services, online support, information, guidance on how to access other resources, and advocacy efforts to change policies and raise awareness about sexual violence.

NATIONAL ORGANIZATION FOR VICTIM ASSISTANCE (WWW.TRYNOVA.ORG)

This site offers supportive resources to survivors, training and education for professionals who work with survivors, and advocates for policy changes.

KNOW YOUR IX (WWW.KNOWYOURIX.ORG)

Know Your IX focuses on advocating for the rights of students who have experienced sexual harassment or sexual violence while on a college campus.

Survivors of Incest Anonymous (siawso.org)

SIA provides a safe and supportive environment and resources for those who experienced incest or childhood sexual abuse.

FORGE (www.forge-forward.org/official)

FORGE (For Ourselves: Reworking Gender Expression) is a national transgender anti-violence organization that provides support and resources to transgender, gender nonconforming, and non-binary individuals who have experienced violence.

National Queer and Trans Therapists of Color Network (nqttcn.com)

This organization focuses on the mental health and therapeutic needs of queer and transgender people of color, including a therapist dictionary, advocacy and awareness, training, support, and resources.

1in6 (Male Survivors) (1in6.org)

1in6 is dedicated to providing support and resources for male survivors of sexual abuse and assault.

LOCAL SUPPORT

In addition to finding support by phone or website, there are also in-person resources available to you. If this is what you prefer but you are not sure how to find an in-person resource, many help hotlines, including the National Sexual Assault Hotline at 1-800-656-HOPE

(4673), can point you toward support agencies in your area. You can also search online with the keywords "sexual assault support" followed by your city or region.

Sexual assault and domestic violence advocacy centers: These are organizations that provide support and assistance to those who have experienced assault by offering services such as counseling, legal advocacy, medical accompaniment, and other resources that may be helpful.

Law enforcement stations: Law enforcement stations can provide information on the reporting process, assist in protection and safety concerns, and the collection of evidence. They can also make referrals to supportive services, provide victim advocates, and offer resources about legal guidance.

Health care centers: Health care centers, such as hospitals and clinics, are safe and confidential environments for you to receive medical care, information about your rights, and information about available support services. A sexual assault forensic examination may also be completed by a professional trained in completing these exams. If the center does not have a trained professional on site, they can provide the names and locations of health care centers that provide this service.

Planned Parenthood clinics: Planned Parenthood is a health care center with a focus on advocacy and support for sexual assault survivors, including pregnancy and STI testing, referrals and information about local resources, and sexual assault education. They provide support to all genders and provide gender-affirming care.

Women's health centers: These are facilities that provide medical services and supports specific to the health care needs of women, including gynecological care, reproductive health services, family planning, education, counseling, and resources related to women's health care.

ADDRESSING YOUR PHYSICAL INJURIES

If you have recently been sexually assaulted and were injured in the assault, it is recommended that you go to the emergency room to receive medical care. The hospital staff will document your injuries and the reason for the visit, both of which can be beneficial for filing a report. At the hospital, you can have evidence collected and ask for support to prevent sexually transmitted infections and pregnancy. Unless you're a minor, whether you decide to file a report is entirely up to you, and you can make that decision at another time. If you're a minor, medical professionals are required to report concerns of abuse to the appropriate authorities (see more information about mandated reporters in chapter five). If weeks or months have passed since the assault, you may still consider having an examination and be tested for pregnancy or sexually transmitted diseases. If it's been years since the assault, and you have lingering health issues that you suspect were caused by the assault, it's a good idea to share your concerns with a health care provider.

SAVE EVIDENCE AND DOCUMENT
THE ASSAULT

You can gather and document evidence of the assault, whether or not you're choosing to report it immediately. This can feel overwhelming, especially when you want to do the opposite and try to forget about what happened. Your response to trauma can make it hard to think clearly about what you just experienced. If you already missed the opportunity to complete some of these steps, that's okay. Be kind to yourself. Just do what you can, and what you feel safe to do, so that you have as much evidence as possible, should you choose to report the assault.

Consider taking photos of the following, if possible:

- the location where the crime occurred,
- any physical injuries you have,
- clothing you were wearing and any rips/tears/marks that resulted from the assault.

Place clothing, sheets, or other associated items in a sealed plastic bag. Contact someone you trust right away and tell them what happened. Offer as many details as you are comfortable with; this potentially offers you a secondary witness later on (a secondary witness is someone who did not directly observe the event, but heard about it from someone who was directly involved). Write down a detailed account of what happened. Think of:

- who was involved (both directly and indirectly),
- where it occurred,
- what happened,
- when it happened.

Email this document to someone you trust, or to yourself, so you have a time stamp. If verbalizing what happened is easier for you than writing about it, record yourself describing your account, and be sure to cover the bullet points above. Save this recording or share it in a way that includes a time stamp. Being as detailed as possible can be helpful, but after experiencing a trauma, it might be hard to recall all the details. That's okay and normal after going through a trauma. Do your best to document as much as you can.

After an assault, many people express feeling "dirty," and it's normal to want to scrub yourself clean. But the best chance for DNA to be collected is for evidence to be gathered within a seventy-two-hour window and with as little contamination as possible. So, if you think you might want to report the crime, go to an emergency room as soon as you can.

Although the window for collecting DNA evidence is open for seventy-two hours after the assault, evidence is better preserved if you get to an ER sooner. If at all possible, avoid using the restroom, combing your hair, changing your clothes, and showering or bathing.

SUPPORT FROM SURVIVORS: WHAT SEXUAL ASSAULT SURVIVORS WANT YOU TO KNOW

I asked sexual assault survivors what they'd want to say to someone who just experienced sexual assault. Here are some of their responses:

"You're safe now."

"I believe you."

"Don't make excuses for the person who assaulted you. It can be tempting to try to make excuses, to understand why they did it. But the blame belongs on them. Not you."

"There is not a rule book that says how you should or shouldn't feel. Any feelings you have are valid."

"Even if you don't mean to, you might victim-blame yourself. Try to recognize when you are doing this and be kind to yourself."

"Don't shower and go ask for help immediately. You can't do
    this alone; it is okay to lean on others."

"Consider getting a rape kit done and look into resources to
    help you to know what to do."

"Keep fighting."

"It wasn't your fault. There's nothing you could have done dif-
    ferently. I'm here for you."

"Trust your gut. You're not crazy. Your body knows what hap-
    pened was wrong."

"Practice self-care for your mental and physical well-being in
    the days after."

CONSIDERING THE OPTION TO REPORT

With the exception of minors, the decision to file a report is yours, and yours alone. It can take time to process the trauma you experienced, and you may not feel ready to report at this time. Some people wait years to report, and some never do. While you may find it comforting that this is your decision to make, making this decision can sometimes add to the stress you're already experiencing.

Some states have a limited timeframe for pressing charges for sexual assault and other crimes. These statutes of limitations are currently being challenged in those states to increase the time limits for survivors of sexual assault. You can check the current statute of limitations for sexual assaults in your state at RAINN.org or get the information from a local sexual assault advocacy center.

When you're weighing the pros and cons of reporting, you don't have to make the decision alone. Hotlines and sexual assault advocacy centers are often good resources to help you learn about your options and provide information for other concerns that you have.

How to Start the Reporting Process

If you know you want to report the assault, here's how to start the process:

1. If you're a minor, you can tell an adult or mandated reporter. Mandated reporters are people who work with youth, such as teachers, counselors, social workers, clergy members, doctors, and nurses, who are required to report crimes against minors. They will help you through the process.

2. If you're an adult, you can go directly to the police station and file a report in person. When you get there, ask to speak with an officer and inform them that you would like to make a sexual assault report.

3. You can call 911 or your local police station and report the assault over the phone.

4. You can also file the report with someone else's assistance. For example, if you go to the hospital for a medical examination, you can tell the health care professional that you want to make a report. Another option is to reach out to your local advocacy center and tell them you would like to make a report.

For detailed information on what to expect when you file a report and how to prepare, jump to chapter five.

Making the decision to report isn't easy, especially while you're processing the trauma, finding your way forward, and working on your healing. So, take the time you need to decide what you want to do next.

It's not fair that you've been put in a position where you've been hurt and have to be so brave and have so many hard choices to make. Taking the time to carefully consider your options can help you to take some of your power back.

I know this is a lot of information to take in and that everything you learn can lead to even more questions. So, if you haven't already made a list of questions that you want to have answered, this is a good time to start.

LET'S CHECK IN

If the trauma is making you feel like you're not in control, here are some things other survivors find helpful to ground themselves and decompress:

- Go outside for at least ten minutes and do some deep breathing.
- Write what you're thinking and feeling in your journal.
- Play uplifting music and move your body.
- Take a warm bubble bath and listen to soft music.
- List five things you can see, four things you can touch, three things you can hear, two things you can smell, and one thing you can taste.
- If you have any pets, spend time with them, talking to them and petting them.

When you're ready, take a deep breath, and we'll dive into the next chapter together.

CHAPTER 3

Additional Steps to Consider Taking
Following an Assault

In the first few days after your assault, you may be looking for ways to restore a sense of safety and control, but you might not feel sure about what's safe and what isn't. You might not even feel safe in your own skin. Some people feel safer and more in control by staying home or staying away from other people. Others feel better getting right back into their regular routines or creating more structure in their lives. For me, it took a long time to find out that my need to stay busy and return to "normal" was a common reaction for some sexual assault victims. At that time, because I was functioning at work and school, and because I believed the myth that people who are assaulted have a visible emotional reaction, I thought I should be able to deal with what happened and didn't immediately ask for help. Had I known more about sexual assault, I believe I'd have looked for support and resources to start my healing journey sooner. And that's my hope for you.

Within the first few days after being assaulted, consider your options to:

- get medical care,
- gather evidence,

- continue the conversation about reporting,
- create a safety plan so you can continue to process the trauma.

MEDICAL CARE AND SEXUAL ASSAULT FORENSIC EXAMINATIONS

Visiting a medical professional may be the last thing you want to do right now, but when we're in crisis or survival mode, we're not always aware of the extent of our injuries or other issues that need to be addressed, so please get the medical attention you deserve.

Another good reason to see a medical provider in the first few days is that they can prescribe a medication to help prevent sexually transmitted infections (STIs). The sooner this medication is started, the more effective it's likely to be.

A third reason to visit a health care professional is to complete a sexual assault forensic exam, sometimes called a rape kit. Having this exam is a powerful action step to assess your condition and document your injuries, which can be useful if you decide to report the crime. During the exam, the health care professional will perform a physical and genital exam and collect evidence. They will also talk with you about sexually transmitted infections and the risk of pregnancy. If you're uncomfortable with certain parts of the exam, tell the health care professional working with you that you'd like to skip those parts.

The professionals completing this examination should be trauma-informed and trained in how to support victims of assault. Ideally, they'll use their training and knowledge when completing the examination, but some survivors have reported experiences where they did not receive the care or support they needed. Most survivors say they *did* get the physical and emotional support they needed, but if your experience is negative, I assure you that the provider's lack of compassion and care is not a reflection on you, and it doesn't make what you went through any less valid.

OPTIONS FOR REPORTING AND COMPLETING THE RAPE KIT

Unless you're a minor, choosing to have a forensic exam doesn't mean that you're also choosing to report the crime (medical professionals are mandated reporters; see page 96). But if you know you want to file a report, you can choose to have an examination and file a report at the same time. Unfortunately, there have been issues with sexual assault examination kits being mishandled or stored without being processed. Ask your victim advocate how the rape kits in your state are handled and for more information about how the evidence will be processed.

> **Sexual assault forensic exam locations.** Call the National Sexual Assault Hotline (800-656-4673) and ask them to direct you to the nearest location, because not all hospitals and clinics are equipped to offer sexual assault forensic examinations.
>
> **You don't have to go to the exam alone.** The examination can take a few hours, so you may want to ask someone to go with you for emotional support. You also have the right to have an advocate with you, as we discussed in the previous chapter. The advocate can help you understand the process, advocate for your rights, and answer your questions. The idea of having an advocate that you don't know being present for the exam may seem uncomfortable, but when we experience a trauma, it can be helpful to have someone there who understands how trauma affects us.

Practitioners that perform the exam. The exam will be done by a doctor, nurse practitioner, physician's assistant, or registered nurse who is certified as a sexual assault nurse examiner (SANE).

You don't have to pay for a rape kit. The crime victims' compensation covers the cost of the examination. When you go to the hospital, you can ask for an advocate or social worker to help you with the paperwork so you're not navigating this alone.

SUPPORT FROM SURVIVORS: WHY MORE PEOPLE DON'T REPORT

The following comments from survivors help to explain why people often feel like they can't or shouldn't report sexual assault.

"He was family and my parents saw it as making the family name look bad."

"I was told it wasn't REALLY assault by my mother, who said her more violent assault was more 'real.'"

"He threatened to harm himself if I told anyone."

"I didn't want to believe that it had happened to me. Reporting made it seem real."

"I was overwhelmed and didn't know where to start."

"I just wanted to try to move forward from it. Reporting would have meant that I had to keep thinking about it."

"They were family."

"I was afraid of being blamed."

"They were a cop."

The Exam: What to Expect

Before going in for the examination, do your best to avoid activities that may destroy evidence, including bathing, using the restroom, changing clothes, combing your hair, or cleaning any part of your body that may have come into contact with the perpetrator. It may not be realistic to avoid all of these activities, but don't let that stop you from moving forward with the examination if you want to have it.

During the exam. The medical professional will start the exam by caring for any injuries that need immediate attention. Next, they'll gather medical history, and some of these questions may be about your previous sexual activity. They ask about people you've recently had consensual sex with because those partners' DNA may show up in the lab report, and they want to make sure that DNA that isn't the perpetrator's is noted in the written report. You will also be asked to share specific information about the assault. If there are questions you're not ready to answer, just tell them as much as you are comfortable with.

After collecting your history, they will do a head-to-toe assessment and gather samples that are appropriate for your specific situation, like urine, blood, and hair—see the following sidebar for details. This assessment will include examining and swabbing parts of your body that were violated during the assault. If you believe you were drugged, you can also ask for a toxicology screening.

During your examination, you can take a break, choose not to do part of the exam, or stop the exam altogether. You're in control. Taking your power back by having evidence gathered gives you more options down the road, but your sense of safety is the highest priority. So if you want to take a break or need to pause, that's perfectly okay and understandable.

If you're a minor (under the age of eighteen), the health care professional who completes the examination will be legally obligated to report the crime to law enforcement and social services. Each state has its own mandatory reporter laws.

EXPERT CONTRIBUTION: FORENSIC EXAMINATIONS AND STI TESTING

Lindsay Nelson, Board Certified Nurse Midwife

Seeking health care and completing follow-up health screenings after a sexual assault can be difficult for survivors, as these encounters often bring up feelings of vulnerability and may be triggering. As health care providers, we strive to make you feel safe, secure, and protected as we care for you.

You will be screened for: chlamydia, gonorrhea, trichomoniasis, yeast, bacterial vaginosis, hepatitis B, syphilis, and HIV.

Presumptive treatment offered includes:

- Antibiotics for chlamydia, gonorrhea, and trichomoniasis. This will consist of an intramuscular injection of ceftriaxone, an oral dose of azithromycin, and an oral dose of metronidazole.
- Administration of the hepatitis B vaccine depends on the hepatitis B vaccine status of the survivor. If the survivor has not previously been vaccinated, both the hepatitis B vaccine and HBIG (hepatitis B immune globulin) are recommended at the initial examination with follow-up hepatitis B vaccine doses at one to two months and four to six months after the first dose. Survivors who were previously vaccinated but who did not receive post-vaccination testing should receive a single vaccine booster dose.
- HPV vaccination is recommended for female survivors aged nine to twenty-six and male survivors aged nine to twenty-one (up to age twenty-six for men who have sex with men [MSM]). The vaccine should be administered at the initial examination, and follow-up doses are administered at one to two months and six months after the first dose.

- Recommendations for HIV post-exposure prophylaxis (PEP) are individualized according to risk.

HOW TO FIND A MEDICAL PROVIDER AND WHAT TO EXPECT DURING A FORENSIC EXAMINATION

Hospital emergency departments work with sexual assault nurse examiners (SANE) to provide sexual assault forensic exams. To find a local sexual assault service provider outside of the emergency department setting, call the National Sexual Assault Hotline at 800-656-HOPE (4673). Forensic exams can be completed in an outpatient clinic setting if you're more comfortable in that environment.

If possible, avoid bathing and showering, using the restroom, changing clothes, combing your hair, and cleaning up the parts of your body that were violated prior to the forensic examination, as doing so could damage potential evidence. In most cases, DNA evidence has to be collected within seventy-two hours to be analyzed by a crime lab, but a forensic exam can reveal other forms of evidence that can be used beyond this timeframe if you decide to report the crime.

Informed consent is essential during a forensic examination. Every step of the examination should be explained to you, and your consent will be obtained prior to beginning the examination. You can stop, pause, or skip any step at any time during the exam.

A sexual assault forensic exam includes the following:

- Immediate care: Any injuries sustained that require immediate attention will be treated first.

- History: You will be asked questions about your current medications and pre-existing health conditions. Some personal questions about recent consensual sexual activities will be asked to ensure that DNA and other evidence collected during the exam can be connected to the perpetrator. You will be asked details about what happened to you so that all potential areas of injury and evidence collection from your body and clothing can be identified.

- Head-to-toe examination: A full body examination, including internal examinations of the mouth, vagina, and/or anus will be completed with your consent. Samples of blood, urine, hair, and swabs of body surface areas will be collected. Photographs will be taken during the exam to document injuries. Physical evidence collected may include your clothing, undergarments, and anything left by the perpetrator such as a torn piece of clothing, stray hair, or debris.

- Possible mandatory reporting: You do not have to report the crime to have a forensic examination, but the process gives you the chance to collect and safely store DNA and evidence should you decide to report at a later time. If the survivor is a minor, there might be mandatory reporting laws per the state laws.

- Follow-up care: You will likely be offered prevention treatment for STIs, and follow-up testing will be recommended. Follow-up care should include mental health care.

FINDING A SENSE OF SAFETY
AFTER THE ASSAULT

Being sexually assaulted can take away your sense of safety and security, so it's important to do whatever you can to feel more secure while you're addressing the trauma with a therapist. At home, consider the following actions:

- change the locks,
- notify friends and family of safety concerns,
- keep all doors and windows locked,
- preprogram your phone with 911 and other emergency numbers,
- change your computer/technology passwords. Factory reset any technology you worry may be compromised, and consider what apps are on your phone that share your location with others.

Here are some safety steps to take in the community:

- keep your phone charged and with you at all times,
- lock your car as soon as you get in or out,
- if you don't feel safe, ask someone to go with you or stay on the phone with you while you do errands,
- speak to an advocate about protection orders, such as emergency or temporary protection orders, sexual assault protection orders, no-contact orders, or long-term protection orders,
- communicate your plans with someone you trust, including when you plan to return home.

TECHNOLOGY SAFETY

The Safety Net Project explores and shares information about technology safety regarding sexual violence and intimate partner violence. This includes a technology toolkit for survivors, which covers:

- basic technology safety,
- how to secure accounts and devices,
- technology and sexual assault,
- teens and technology,
- stalkerware and location tracking,
- phone safety and security,
- online privacy and safety,
- personal information and data privacy,
- data security,
- internet and connected devices,
- and app safety.

Visit www.TechSafety.org to see the full resource and updated content.

EXPERT CONTRIBUTION: UNDERREPORTING OF SEXUAL ASSAULT IN THE NATIVE AMERICAN/ALASKAN NATIVE POPULATION[10,11,12]

Lalania Walker, White Earth Tribal Child Advocacy Center Coordinator

As a Native American/Alaskan Native person in the United States, I know the victimization of sexual violence has been rampant, originating from colonialism and a long history of violence spanning back centuries. Sara Deer, professor at William Mitchell College of Law, listened to stories of Indigenous women who have identified themselves as fifth-generation sexual assault survivors. Collecting comprehensive data on statistics such as rape, sexual abuse, etc., for the Native

American/Alaskan Native population has been uncommon. Recently, there have been more efforts to collect data on such statistics, reiterating the high prevalence of rape and sexual violence Native American/Alaskan Native people face.

Adult

In 1998, the National Violence Against Women Survey collected an alarming statistic, that one in three Native women will be raped in their lifetime, which resulted in policy reform, investigative reporting, etc. More recent numbers have been collected in 2023, representing data from adult male and female survivors of sexual assault. Compared to all races, Native Americans/Alaskan Native people are twice as likely to experience rape/sexual assault. When categorizing sexual violence statistics by gender, 56.1 percent of Native American/Alaskan Native women experience sexual violence and 27.5 percent Native American/Alaskan Native men experience sexual violence according to the US Department of Justice National Institute of Justice, 2023.

Children

Although prevalence of child sexual abuse in Native American/Alaskan Native populations is unknown, due to child victims not disclosing their abuse, approximate rates of abuse can be deduced from other reports. Specifically, the Centers for Disease Control and Prevention reported that one in four women and one in six men in the general population were sexually abused before the age of eighteen, and the US Department of Health and Human Services report found that Native American/Alaskan Native children are two times more likely to be victims of child sexual abuse when compared to Caucasian children. Together this information suggests that two in four Native women and two in six Native men have been sexually abused before the age of eighteen. When looking deeper into the underreporting of child sexual abuse, 73 percent of child victims do not disclose within the first year, 45 percent of victims do not disclose within at least five years, and some child victims never disclose.[13,14]

Underreporting

Victims of sexual assault chose not to report their assault to the police for various reasons, which included: feared retaliation, believing the police would not do anything to help, and some believed that their assault was not important enough to report. When focusing on the Native American/Alaskan Native population in regard to underreporting, there are layers of mistrust with the system and institutions, and other historical factors that unfortunately exacerbate underreporting of sexual assault.

While considering America's violent past toward the Indigenous population, rape and sexual assault were embedded in the efforts to assimilate and destroy Indigenous communities. Whether you are looking at how rampant sexual assault was in boarding schools across North America and beyond or looking at how men who worked for the US government raped women and girls as young as twelve years old while they were forced to walk the Trail of Tears, perpetrators were not held accountable, and often still received salaries and support while carrying out abuse. When perpetrators are not held accountable, unfortunately, victims may develop a learned silence, or internalize not challenging authority, learn to devalue their safety and personal boundaries, and become accustomed to living in abusive environments.

Time and time again, Native American and Alaskan Native children cry out about sexual abuse, and nothing is done to hold perpetrators accountable. Sometimes there are jurisdictional loopholes that result in a perpetrator walking free, or little was done in an investigation, resulting in dropped charges and a closed case. If the unfortunate event happens that they are sexually abused again, it is very unlikely that they will try to report again or want to engage in another investigation.

Native American/Alaskan Native children and adults may be reluctant to disclose sexual abuse due to the nature of the communal culture they belong to. When an individual has a communal culture background, they care about their community's well-being versus their individual well-being. When one has an individual cultural background, they tend to care more about their individual well-being over their community's well-being. From this perspective a Native American/Alaskan Native child may be reluctant to disclose or recant disclosure as they consider their family or community well-being over their own well-being.

Maybe their uncle is the perpetrator, and he helps their mom pay the bills. Maybe their stepsister is the perpetrator, and the child victim does not want to upset or separate their parents. These are situations to consider if the perpetrator is a family member; familial reactions may influence reluctance or a recantation. Furthermore, Indigenous families rely on one another, and family is a high value. Often Indigenous families reside in multigenerational households, and there is a high level of poverty in the Native American/Alaskan Native population, which may add more pressure to a child victim to be reluctant or recant their disclosure of sexual assault. In addition, if the perpetrator is a well-respected member of the community, a spiritual adviser or community leader, reluctance may be present.

VAWA

The Violence Against Women Act (VAWA) is a federal law that comprehensively addresses violence such as stalking, sexual assault, domestic violence, and dating violence by focusing on funding, criminal justice system reform, and program development. VAWA encourages a community-coordinated response to violence and has improved the federal, tribal, state, and local response to these crimes. VAWA has allotted funding streams to tribal sexual assault and domestic violence programs.

Since VAWA was passed in 1994, the law has been remanded and reauthorized four times. In each reauthorization, Native American and Alaska Native women advocated and fought for the justice, rights, and safety of Native American people, ensuring that their voices were heard. One of the issues was that Native American survivors could not seek justice because tribal courts were not allowed to prosecute non-Native offenders, even when the crime was committed on tribal lands. The 2013 VAWA reauthorization gave tribal courts the authority to hold offenders accountable in their tribal communities.

VAWA is an example of the government giving more resources to tribes and Indigenous-focused victim service programs. Justice can take many forms, and healing can look different for everyone, especially for Native people. It is important to remember that you are not alone, you are believed, and this is not your fault. You are not defined by your trauma, and you have thousands of ancestors who walk behind you. There are many Indigenous-focused programs that will assist you, whether they are national hotlines or local tribal programs.

Resources

StrongHearts Native Helpline. A nationwide 24/7 confidential and anonymous culturally-appropriate domestic and sexual violence helpline for Native Americans. StrongHearts advocates offer services at no cost.

- Phone number: 1-844-7NATIVE (762-8483)
- Website for a live chat: https://strongheartshelpline.org/

- Services offered:
  - ○ Peer support and advocacy
  - ○ Information and education about domestic violence and sexual violence
  - ○ Personalized safety planning
  - ○ Crisis intervention
  - ○ Referrals to Native-centered domestic violence and sexual violence service providers
  - ○ Basic information about health options
  - ○ Support finding a local health facility or crisis center trained in the care of survivors of sexual assault and forensic exams
  - ○ General information about jurisdiction and legal advocacy referrals

KEEP THE CONVERSATION GOING AROUND REPORTING

It's not unusual for sexual assault victims to feel conflicted about whether or not to report the crime. Some people want to feel absolutely certain that reporting is, or is not, the right thing to do beforehand, and unfortunately that certainty can be hard to come by.

Survivors often don't report because:

- we don't know if anyone will believe us,
- we're confused about what happened,
- we know our perpetrator and feel guilty reporting them,
- we're afraid of the legal process.

Let's break these down a bit more.

You don't know if anyone will believe you. Unfortunately, because of sexual assault myths and misconceptions, there's a good chance that some people won't believe you've been assaulted. But there *are* communities that will believe and support you. Consider connecting with a local or online support group that can help you to figure out what's best for *you*. And keep searching for supports who believe you.

You're confused about what happened. Feeling confused or disoriented after an assault isn't uncommon, especially if your experience conflicts with a sexual assault myth like, "It wasn't assault if you know the person who did it," "It wasn't assault if there wasn't a weapon," or any of the other myths. Because of myths, gaslighting, and the wide spectrum of trauma responses, it's not unusual for victims to wonder if what happened was, in fact, an assault. If you've had consensual sexual encounters, it can be helpful to remember that you didn't look back at those experiences with doubt.

You know your perpetrator and feel guilty reporting them. It's time to dismiss the idea that rapists are monsters hiding in dark alleys. Unfortunately, they're often people we know and may even be people we have feelings for or care about. They may be someone we're related to, and even part of our immediate family. That does not excuse what they did. You're not reporting them because you believe they are a horrific person through and through. You're reporting them for doing something reprehensible and illegal. They should be held accountable for the trauma and crime they inflicted.

You're afraid of the legal process. The legal process is far from perfect, and it can be intimidating, but it's slowly improving with the advocacy efforts of survivors and allies alike. For example, one of the improvements is that many states are lengthening or eliminating the window of time that victims have to report, called the statute of limitations.

If you want to report, but you're afraid or anxious about the process, reach out to resources such as victim advocates or communities like We Are the Evidence.

SUPPORT FROM SURVIVORS:
FEELING SAFE AND FEELING READY TO REPORT

Survivors shared the following suggestions for what friends and family could do to help them feel safe enough to report their sexual assault. It's okay to ask for this support from those closest to you.

"Recognize that assault is assault; lack of consent is all that matters."

"Don't talk about it like it is taboo."

"I wish someone had reassured me that it wasn't normal what they did to me, and that it wasn't my fault."

"Encourage and support me."

"Create open dialogue. If there had been open dialogue before, the door to talking about it and reporting would have already been open."

"Listen and believe me."

"Be there. Be present. Listen and validate my existence and my experience."

"If our mutual friends hadn't been so neutral, I would have felt like reporting was an option."

Celeste's Story

For years I found myself unexpectedly feeling unsafe or uncharacteristically anxious for no apparent reason. I would push the feelings aside and move on. But the feeling lingered and could take days to shake. I called it the "sideways smackdown." I finally started paying closer attention, instead of forcibly ignoring it. What did I think/see/hear/smell just before the feeling? I started identifying patterns of self-talk that triggered self-doubt. Now I could start taking "response-ability." Instead of pushing past the feelings I now acknowledged them. "Hmm. I am feeling really sad all of a sudden. What changed? Oh! I just got a call, and they were raising their voice. It's okay for me to feel sad about that. I'm curious what else it might be triggering. Maybe it was this, or that. I'm not sure, but the good news is that is not happening now." I used affirmations like, "I am safe. I am now. I am ready for the fullness of life I was born for." It wasn't overnight, but the sideways smackdowns became less and less frequent.

Today I have a thriving family of my own, and I am surrounded by love. I travel the world and speak in front of thousands. In fact, I am the founder of the global award-winning nonprofit Days for Girls. We work for a world when periods will never be a problem for anyone, and so far we have helped more than 3 million women and girls in 145 countries have access to menstrual health care products and women's health education. Sincerely, many of the strengths that I have now grew out of overcoming the traumas that I have been through and made me the leader I am today. But it took time and healing, and that healing came as I sought out and took on my healing journey.

Some of the most effective tools for healing that I used were prayer, journaling, free-writing letters (writing quickly without editing or worrying about legibility) to those who had harmed me and then burning the letters. This allowed me to "say my piece" without the need to encounter anyone. Meditation and a strong practice of finding and focusing on gratitude are also very helpful.

I have developed a method that I call "Mind the Gap," which is simple but powerful. It is based on the understanding that there is a moment between when something happens to us and when we interpret what it means to us, and that gap holds tremendous potential for us. There is energy and power that we can take back. We can revisit it and decide, are we going to allow the moment to be demeaning, deforming, undermining, or are we going to get curious about how we can reinterpret it for our own growth and understanding? And could we possibly decide that it is none of our business why the perpetrator did what they did? After all, we cannot be responsible for their actions; we never were. But we can choose for ourselves that we will affirm the strength it took for the survivor in us to go on. That we are proud of the survivor and from this place in time we can choose to let go of the energetic tie to that event and take back our energy for the now. Ignoring it doesn't help. We know and can feel it is there. But "changing the dream," feeling the fear briefly and changing it to you being in control now—that works!

Feel the smackdown when that wave comes, and try stopping long enough to get curious, look at the feeling and where it came from, and reframe your interpretation. Yes! I did go through that. No, it was not my fault. Yes, it was horrible. And yes, I have wisdom and strength that I can share with others. Someday. For right now, this is what I know . . . And add the hope and love that you didn't feel then from the safety of this moment and the growth of now.

We can survive hard things. We already have. But better yet, we can survive and thrive. The future your heart yearns for is not only possible, but important. Go ahead. Dream big.

—Celeste Mergens, Founder of Days for Girls International, author of *The Power of Days: A Story of Resilience, Dignity, and the Fight for Women's Equity*

LET'S CHECK IN

Take a moment to acknowledge yourself for learning more about what you can do, and give yourself a lot of credit for the steps you're already taking.

Whether or not you want to, or are able to report at this time, consider taking the following steps:

- Visit RAINN.org and look at the statutes of limitations in your state. Write them down.
- Look up the name and number of one local advocacy resource. This will be helpful to have, so you know a local place to go to for help when you are ready.
- Write down one reason to consider reporting your assault, and one barrier that may keep you/has kept you from doing so.

CHAPTER 4

Checking In and Understanding the Aftermath of Sexual Assault

Many survivors feel like there's a version of themself who existed before the assault, and a different version after the assault. The trauma can make it seem like our first life has ended and we're starting over as a different person. But even if it seems like you'll never be able to re-integrate the before and after versions, by getting the support you need, you *can* do it. After years of work—on myself and in support of survivors—I've realized that while the assault was a defining experience, it doesn't define who I am. It's my choice to invest in myself and to heal that defines me. If I could go back and talk to myself after I was assaulted, I would encourage that younger version of me to start addressing the pain and beginning the healing process as soon as possible, and I encourage you to do this, too.

PROCESS YOUR RESPONSES TO THE TRAUMA

Survivors of sexual assault don't choose how their mind and body respond to the trauma. We may want to believe that if someone assaults us, we'll use what we learned from true crime documentaries and think quickly to escape or stop the assault. The reality is that when we're faced with something that puts us at risk, it can be very hard to think clearly about anything, including how to respond. So, no matter how hard you fought or didn't fight, it's not your fault. Many survivors are initially upset about their trauma response, and if that's one of the things you're struggling with, I hope learning more about trauma responses and hearing from other survivors will help you to better understand what happened.

Five Trauma Responses: Fight, Flight, Freeze, Flop, Fawn

If you recall the times you've seen someone jump out and scare someone else as a joke, you know they can respond a variety of ways. Some people might have jumped or automatically punched, some might have run, and others may have frozen. People typically don't choose how they will respond in a high-stress situation. Even if you're a professional who's been trained to respond to high-stress situations, the way you respond in a real crisis, or in a crisis that's different from the one you were trained for, can't be predicted.

You've probably heard of the fight-or-flight trauma responses, but there are also three lesser-known trauma responses: freeze, flop, and fawn.

The **fight response** is when we attempt to confront and stop the attacker. Fighting back seems like it would be an automatic response for everyone, but it's not always the way our brain and nervous system respond. As the mind and body work together to try to keep us alive, our response may be very different from what we imagined we might do. Our responses come from our evolution; we behave in ways that worked to help us survive in the past, and we don't have control over this behavior. So, although we may have been able to change the outcome by fighting, evolution may play a role in stopping us from fighting to increase our chances of survival.[15]

In the **flight response**, our stress hormones encourage us to run away from the danger or hide—whatever will create distance or a barrier between us and the person attempting to harm us.

The **freeze response** is when the body becomes tense and silent when faced with a trauma. Research has shown that the freeze response is particularly common in sexual assaults and that this reaction can lead to more doubt and confusion for the victim if they blame themselves for not running away or fighting back.[16] But the mind and body have an incredible ability to assess dangerous situations and respond quickly in order to keep us safe. If running away doesn't seem to be an option and fighting can escalate the violence or increase danger, the sympathetic nervous system may choose to freeze. This response may make the victim feel numb or unaware of what's happening. (The perpetrator's legal defense may use this against the victim, because jury members are often unaware of the different trauma responses.)

The **flop response** is very similar to the freeze response, but instead of freezing and becoming tense, the body may become loose and "floppy." This reaction can be the combined effort of the body and mind to reduce the pain or injury that a victim may experience. With this response the mind also may "tune out" or "shut down" to dissociate from the trauma and make you less aware of what's happening.

When there are signs that a situation may become dangerous, the brain may decide that complying with the threat is the best way to stay safe, avoid escalation, and get some sense of control back from the abuser. This **fawn** response is particularly common when there's an imbalance of power, including when:

- children are assaulted by a parent or other authority figure,
- employees are assaulted by a boss or coworker with power,
- people are assaulted in a marriage or intimate relationship,
- people are threatened with extreme violence,
- human trafficking victims are involved.

Also called the "pleasing" response or the "friend" response, the fawn response can be common among people who experienced long-term abuse as children. Consider a child who is unable to escape their abuser, and over time they learn that by paying attention to changes in their abuser's mood they can attempt to appease them before they escalate to violence.

Survivors who respond this way sometimes blame themselves or fear they won't be believed because they didn't respond with one of the better-known fight-or-flight responses and because they acted in ways that seem counterintuitive based on incorrect ideas about sexual assault responses, but more survivors are becoming aware of this response and openly discussing it.

No matter how your body and brain responded, what happened wasn't your fault.

If you fought with everything you had but were still overpowered, that's not your fault.

If you tried to run away but couldn't, that's not your fault.

If fighting or fleeing didn't seem like safe options, that's not your fault.

If your automatic survival response was to comply and attempt to please, that's not your fault.

EXPERT CONTRIBUTION: ENDING THE STIGMA OF THE FRIEND TRAUMA RESPONSE

Lauren Weingarten, Credentialed Victim Advocate and Certified Trauma Support Specialist

Content Warning: Discussion/Story of sexual assault

I kept thinking how scared I was for him to wake up. Would he remember what he had done to me the night before? What would he say? What would I say? Would he do it to me all over again? What would the morning bring? As the sun started to come up, I was still trying to make sense and piece together the events from the hours prior—events that I couldn't even process in privacy or safety. I felt this fear that I had never quite felt before, this nauseating, full-body fear that was felt by every nerve in me.

So somewhere in the next few hours, unable to process the events that had happened and faced with seemingly only bad options, my survivor brain thought of the most genius plan of all genius plans! If I couldn't fight him or report him, the threat still needed to be addressed. In that shell-shocked state, I decided the best thing to do would be to try and have sex with him when he woke up. At the time, the plan made so much sense. I think that I thought that if we had sex, somehow it would erase what had happened the night before. I intuitively thought that maybe if I agreed and consented now, it would retroactively count as my consent for last night, erasing the horrible memories and thoughts flashing around in my head. I didn't want to keep feeling like I had been feeling.

Instinctively, I decided that this time with me not only consenting but initiating, I could take away the pain and the injustice I had pulsing through me from the previous night's encounter. I was returning to the scene of the crime. But this time, I thought that I was in control. I felt like if we could have sex, then it could keep him from hurting me. I thought that if I gave him what I thought he wanted, he wouldn't have to try and take it from me. The plan made me feel a small sense of relief from worrying what he would do when he woke up. I also thought that it would make it less weird and nerve-racking to see him at work. I felt more confident about my ability to be able to walk away without further incidents of harm.

Every fiber of my being felt like I had to try to forget this ever happened in order to be able to function and move forward. What I didn't see then, but see so clearly now, is that I was doing what I needed to do to survive and protect myself from that horrible experience.

You may be familiar with the concept of "fight-or-flight" responses, but two less talked about trauma responses are freeze and fawn/appease. While not as well known, freeze and fawn are both just as valid and documented.

When we feel either a perceived or real threat, our "rational" brain goes offline and our limbic system takes over. The limbic system is our survival brain. Our limbic system will respond by either fighting, fleeing, freezing, fawning, or some combination of those responses. Faster than you can imagine, our brains will automatically try to evaluate and analyze the facts of the current situation while scanning past experiences and memories like a database to help decide the best option.

Let's say you're walking down the street and you see a bear. You don't know if you could fight or flee, so you may become frozen, unable to move or take action. Maybe you try to befriend the bear in hope of alleviating the threat and to be able to pass safely through. That's the appease/fawn response.

We wouldn't judge someone for how they reacted after facing the bear, so we shouldn't judge when facing other threats to our survival such as a sexual assault. We do what we need to do to survive, and we don't choose how our bodies will let us respond to those threats.

I didn't know it then, but I now know that it is actually not uncommon for survivors to have consensual encounters with their abusers after an assault or horrific episode. In an effort to regain control, to retroactively consent and try to change our ill-fated outcome, we sometimes do things that on the surface do not make any sense to others, things that make our pain and experiences seem insignificant or perhaps even made up. After all, this isn't how survivors are "supposed" to act.

But for every person who is able to recognize and walk away from abuse immediately, there are more like me, who unconsciously try to appease or fix the problem because that is what our brains have been trained to do. For some people, that "fawn" response may very well be the only way our brains can try to cope with the enormity of what has happened to us.

People react to and cope with traumatic events in a multitude of ways. Your current emotional state, age, culture, your support system, genetics, past traumas, your relationship to your attacker—all of those factors play a part. As I would later be told a plethora of times, there is no wrong way to react to trauma. It is our bodies and minds reacting normally to an abnormal situation. It is not a judgment of our character.

Some people may have a clear and firm understanding of their assault and take the immediate steps to advocate for their bodies and themselves. For others, like myself, it is not that clear-cut. And both and everything in between are okay. All of those reactions are valid.

All I wanted was for this night not to have happened and for no one to find out. I felt humiliated and scared for my safety. I just wanted my regular life back. My survival brain presented this as a safe option.

SUPPORT FROM SURVIVORS: TRAUMA RESPONSES

While healing from sexual assault, it's helpful to connect with other survivors and know that you're not alone in how you responded to your assault. You may not have connected with a community of sexual assault survivors yet, but here are some responses that other survivors have shared about the impact their assault had on them.

"I felt betrayed by my body. Why wasn't I screaming?"

"Freezing made me feel shame, like a 'real man' would have fought."

"Freezing makes me think that is why the authorities didn't take me seriously."

"My fawn response confused me and contributed to me staying with my rapist for years."

"I tried to fight but was unsuccessful and then froze, and then fawned."

"I tried to get away, but he pinned me down so I couldn't escape and I froze."

"I am happy I tried to fight, but my freeze response that kicked in when fighting didn't work caused me a lot of guilt."

"I felt like it was my fault for not fighting harder."

"Even though I tried to escape, the fact that I wasn't strong enough to made me ashamed and guilty."

"I have a lot of self-hatred and regular nightmares and flashbacks from my trauma. The freezing specifically made it worse."

"You are taught to question yourself and your choices as a victim. I felt guilty for my response to the trauma."

"I felt super-guilty and ashamed. I still do and it's been four years."

"Freezing caused guilt, because I felt as if I implied consent."

"Freezing caused me to not believe it was rape and that I was dramatic."

"Freezing made me doubt the severity of what happened to me and regret not fighting for myself."

"I tried to run away, and he grabbed my arm. That traumatized me."

"My freeze response made me more numb and caused a lack of self-esteem."

"Me fighting back caused the assault to be more violent, hence me getting more physically hurt."

"I felt like my body betrayed me. I didn't feel human anymore."

"My response caused me pain because I didn't react how I thought I would in that situation."

"My freeze did cause a lot of guilt, and I tried to rationalize the assault for a long time because of it."

"My freezing is what the defense used against me in court to victim-blame me."

"I thought my response was normal, and I continued to be in abusive relationships."

"I now still freeze daily on things that I shouldn't."

"I froze at first but then started to fight back."

"It took me a long time to realize it was rape, since I didn't fight back. I doubted myself."

"I fought verbally but not physically. I felt like I could have done more."

'The way I responded caused me a lot of guilt and depression."

"I felt so much regret, anger, guilt, confusion, and numbness."

"It made it hard for me to accept that it was sexual assault because I didn't fight back."

"I felt guilt about freezing and minimized my assault because of that."

"I felt like I couldn't report because I didn't fight him off."

Defense Mechanisms

Defense mechanisms are coping practices we use (knowingly or unknowingly) to decrease our anxiety or emotional reaction to stressful events. Defense mechanisms can be helpful at times, but they can also be maladaptive and delay the healing process.

Avoidance: We try to avoid situations that cause us to feel distress. For example, after experiencing assault you may avoid driving near the location where the assault occurred.

Compensation: If we think we have a weakness, we may try to enhance our strengths to make up for it. For example, after assault you may not feel strong or that you were not strong enough to defend yourself and may throw yourself into fitness routines and self-defense classes to counteract that feeling.

Conversion: When we have physical symptoms due to a stress that does not have a medical cause. After sexual assault, you may experience severe physical symptoms, even though there are no identifiable physical injuries or medical causes for the symptoms. These symptoms are related to the emotional pain you are experiencing.

Denial: The refusal to acknowledge or accept a situation, denial is a coping mechanism and is often named as one of the stages of grief. Denial is common for those who have survived trauma because, in addition to processing the trauma, they're grieving the life they had before the assault.

Displacement: When we direct our negative feelings onto someone other than the person we're actually upset with. Often, this will be toward something or someone we have more power over. For example, when someone has a stressful day at work they may snap at their partner or overreact to small annoyances.

Dissociation and depersonalization: These can be the result of post-traumatic stress disorder and lead a person to feel distant from themselves, or like they're floating above or watching themselves from a distance. **Derealization** is similar to dissociation, but with derealization someone might also feel detached from their surroundings. People also describe feeling disconnected from their emotions, actions, and memories when they're dissociating.

Identification: When someone adopts someone else's traits or behaviors. For example, after an assault, a survivor may begin to look and act more like a family member that they consider "tough" by adopting that person's beliefs and routines.

Projection: When we place our thoughts or feelings onto someone else without realizing it. For example, someone may assume that other people share their opinions or beliefs.

Rationalization: When we attempt to explain or justify behaviors with logic. We try to think through our feelings rather than truly experience the emotions we're having.

Reaction formation: When we express feelings that are the opposite of what we truly feel because we believe our emotions are inappropriate or will cause more anxiety if we show them. For example, you may internally feel intense rage toward your assailant, as well as feelings of guilt and self-blame, but externally you show excessive compassion toward your assailant.

Regression: When we revert to earlier developmental behaviors. This is sometimes a sign that a child is being sexually abused. An example of a child regressing might be a child who was potty trained suddenly wetting the bed again. Adults may regress also. This may look like throwing a tantrum and refusing to do things requested of them.

Repression: An involuntary response to block out painful memories or emotions. For example, you may not be able to recall details of the assault when asked about it during the reporting process.

Splitting: Being unable to see "gray areas" in people or in conflicts; they become black or white, all or nothing. For example, after experiencing assault by a man, you see all men as potential threats and do not trust any of them, while also believing all women are innocent and could never cause you harm.

Suppression: A voluntary choice to block out thoughts and emotions. Suppression is the same as repression, with the difference being that it is a choice to suppress memories of the assault and the emotions related to it.

Undoing: Trying to cancel out negative behaviors by doing things that are kind or helpful. For example, a partner who shows up with flowers after being violent, believing this will undo the bad behavior.

SUPPORT FROM SURVIVORS: IF YOU QUESTION YOUR TRAUMA RESPONSE

That same community of survivors that wants you to know you're not alone in how your trauma response can impact you also wants to share some encouragement and wisdom.

"It is not at all your fault. You can't take blame for an action they chose to do."

"There is no correct way to respond to trauma. Process your feelings at your own pace."

"Don't feel shameful. It is the rapist's shame to carry, not yours. Stay strong!"

"It's okay if you froze or didn't react. Don't blame yourself and stay strong!"

"Your response did NOT cause the action of the perpetrator. They chose their actions."

"You know the truth and you know it wasn't your fault. You are worthy of love and self-love."

"How you responded was an unconscious response that comes from evolution and assessing danger and survival."

"Freezing and fawning are natural responses, but now you're in control and will heal."

"It really isn't your fault. Even if you froze. It is ALWAYS the rapist's fault."

"Nothing is wrong with you. You are beautiful."

"It's totally normal. It's not always how they paint it in the movies or news."

"You did everything you could. You did nothing wrong. You fought back by surviving."

"Sometimes reality is different than what you expect. Your response in the moment was NOT your fault."

"There is no right way to respond during an attack. Also, talk to someone about it!"

"It wasn't your fault. There is no such thing as the 'perfect rape/assault.'"

"Honestly, I am still working through this myself. Hardest part is to be around people who don't understand. So find people who do!"

"Even if a lot of people act like they don't understand, there
    are a lot of people who do."
"The only important thing is you survived, and you are learn-
    ing how to survive now."
"It's instinctive, so even if you're not able to follow the logic of
    your response, it doesn't mean it was wrong."
"Talk to someone trusted and tell them what happened."
"How you respond to your trauma doesn't define you."
"It's not your fault. You are winning by living!"
"You have the right to feel however you feel."
"Educate, educate, educate yourself!"

FINDING A TRAUMA-INFORMED THERAPIST

Therapy has many benefits, including identifying triggers, processing your trauma, creating goals for yourself, and having support with navigating your trauma. Therapy sessions vary greatly depending on the type of therapy you're trying (see chapter twelve). In general, you can expect therapy to include:

- An initial assessment to gather information about your background, current challenges and stressors, and goals for therapy.
- Time spent to build rapport.
- Setting goals together for your therapy sessions.
- Emotional support.
- Reflection and insight into your thoughts, feelings, and behaviors.

Finding the right therapist can feel overwhelming under any circumstances, but for those in the aftermath of a trauma, it can be especially daunting. Start by thinking about the qualities you want the therapist to have. What follow are some questions to ask when you're vetting therapists.

- Do you have experience with people who were sexually assaulted?
- What is your educational background?
- What topics do you specialize in?
- What area of your work are you most passionate about?
- Do you set goals in therapy?
- How do you gauge progress?
- Do you accept my insurance?
- What are your fees? Do you offer a sliding scale based on what people can afford?

EXPERT CONTRIBUTION: GROUNDING AND COPING SKILLS
Patricia Bathory, MBA, MACP, CCC

Research studies have shown that healthy coping strategies make a significant difference in sexual assault survivors' quality of life. Healthy coping skills, sometimes called active coping strategies, modify the nature of whatever is causing stress or shift the way a survivor views the stressor. A study conducted by the Department of Psychiatry of the Pushpagiri Institute of Medical Sciences and Research Centre in Kerala, India, showed that active coping strategies helped rape survivors to heal and move forward, and avoidant coping strategies, including substance use and denial, "prevent them from directly addressing traumatic events."[17]

Here are some active coping strategies you can try. Their effectiveness will vary from person to person, because no two people are the same and no two stories are the same. You can read through these and circle the ones you feel could be helpful for you. Then try to commit to actively working on at least one of your circled options.

Active Coping Strategies for Your Body

- Calm your body—take deep breaths focusing on the expansion of your chest as you inhale and on its deflation as you exhale. This is very effective both when you're feeling overwhelmed (with physical symptoms), and as an introduction to a meditative reflective state. Try to do this twice a day. Even if you only practice for five minutes twice a day, you will feel the benefits of being present and in tune with your body. Try to extend it to ten to fifteen minutes twice a day, or as needed.

- Find an outlet for anger and other emotions that you want to express. Some people find that physical activity can be particularly soothing, including running, working out, and taking a self-defense course. Anger is a normal response to assault, and since it generates energy, the idea is to use it as fuel for productive and positive activities.

- Reach out to an individual or group of people who have or are healing from sexual assault. Having a connection with someone who can relate and who has seen the other side is very beneficial to increase hope. When you're ready, try to meet them in person, outside where the light shines. Go for a walk or for coffee. Do some type of "everyday" activity in person.

Active Coping Strategies for Your Mind

- Manage negative, intrusive thoughts, which are thoughts that are uninvited and tend to occur at the most inconvenient times. Try to create a space between you and your thoughts. Acknowledge the thought, but remind yourself that you have power to change it, and then replace it with a helpful thought.
- Find the words that describe what happened, your feelings, and the narrative of your story and write about it in your journal or diary.
- Focus on your inner strength or spirituality by meditating, practicing your faith, praying, or whatever activities you find most healing.
- Repeat essential affirmations like:
  - "I am not defined by what happened to me."
  - "Bad things happen to good people for no reason."
  - "I am strong and capable of moving forward."
- Find a psychotherapist with whom you have a good rapport. A qualified and experienced therapist will respect your time, your pace, and your boundaries. You can talk as much or as little as you'd like. I've seen a sexual assault victim who spent her initial four sessions crying, unable to speak a word. She needed a safe place to mourn, and to feel the sadness and anger of what had happened. Once she was ready, she started her healing journey.

CHECKING IN AND SELF-CARE

Checking in with yourself and practicing self-care after sexual assault is crucial for healing and well-being. It involves listening to your emotional and physical needs and engaging in activities that promote self-nurturing.

Physical Health

After an assault, it's not unusual to feel sluggish, tense, or disgusted by your body. You may feel driven to work out, or barely have the energy to get out of bed. There's no right way to feel, but it's helpful to be in touch with whatever we *are* feeling, so take a moment to check in with your body and what it's telling you that it needs.

Taking care of your body can be the first small step in taking back control, especially when you're emotionally struggling. Being intentional about the foods you eat in order to fuel your body and moving your body are some ways to start. This can be through yoga, walking outside, lifting weights, or whatever appeals to you. It can be broken down even further to help you to shower, brush your teeth, and complete your skin care routine.

Physical Self-Check:
- Have I bathed or showered today? If that seems overwhelming, can I wash my face and underarms with a washcloth?
- Have I changed clothes today?
- How much water have I drunk today?
- What have I eaten in the last twenty-four hours?
- In what way can I move my body today while feeling safe?
- Where am I holding tension?
- Does my head hurt?
- Am I clenching my jaw?
- How much sleep am I getting?

Emotional Health

Your emotions are likely to be all over the place and your reactions may not be aligned with what you thought they might be. Sometimes the flood of emotions is so complex, it's hard to find words for what you're feeling. It can be particularly challenging when you're feeling many emotions at the same time and when some of them conflict with each other. For example, you might feel anxious and guilty, but also grateful to be in a safe place. It can be tempting to deny or hide negative feelings, but it's more helpful to acknowledge the feelings and express them in a healthy and safe way. Consider working with a feelings chart to help you sort out how you're feeling and to find words to express those feelings to others or in your journal. A feelings chart can be helpful because it's a visual way to identify emotions. Since our emotions are complex, it's possible to feel many at once, and we don't always have the words to identify the emotions we're feeling. Being able to look at a chart of emotions and reflect can be a helpful step in healing. One good example of a feelings chart is the Feeling Wheel by Gloria Willcox. This is a widely used tool and can be found by searching "the feeling wheel by Gloria Willcox" online.

Here's a list of journal prompts and an exercise to help you release emotions. These prompts can also help you to assess where you are on your healing journey with regard to your emotional health:

- What emotions am I holding on to from my trauma?
- How has my trauma affected my behaviors and thoughts?
- Where would I like to see myself on my healing journey in six months? One year? Five years? Seven years?
- When and where do I feel the most at peace, even if it isn't a complete feeling of peace? What is it about that environment that helps me feel that way?

- What would I like to say to a future version of myself?
- What challenges did I face today, and how did I overcome them?
- What am I in control of in this moment?
- What words of support do I need to hear most?

How to Release Emotions

Here are some ideas for physically releasing emotions. Before attempting these, consult with your health care team to be sure you're not at risk for any injury:

- move your body—run, CrossFit, power lifting,
- get a deep tissue massage,
- breathe, meditate, and try yoga,
- dance,
- be still, notice your emotions, consider what they are telling you, thank them and then let them go,
- make noise: sing, yell, cheer, cry.

Relationships

Relationships, formal supports, and community groups and networks can all play a helpful role in your healing. Consider how different relationships can support you in moving forward. Also think about the people you'd like to connect with for reasons other than assault support, like the aunt you enjoy thrift shopping with or your friend who's a great hiking companion. Connecting with people we enjoy is one of the most beneficial things we can do for ourselves. Use the following chart as a way to recall and write down relationships that you have in your life.

Category:	Family	Friends	Organizations (formal supports/ paid people)	Informal supports in the community (coworkers, hobby connections)
People who are very close to you, and are involved at a daily level, with whom you feel safe. These are your closest relationships.				
People to whom you could reach out if needed, even if you are not in daily contact.				
People who might be able to offer support. Get creative; consider people or organizations that you have some or no contact with but know could be an option.				

An example:

Category:	Family	Friends	Organizations (formal supports/paid people)	Informal supports in the community (coworkers, hobby connections)
People who are very close to you, and are involved at a daily level, with whom you feel safe. These are your closest relationships.		My best friend. She checks in with me daily and always offers support.		My bandmates. They don't know the details of what I am going through but check in and encourage me to practice with them.

| People to whom you could reach out if needed, even if you are not in daily contact. | My parents. Even though we don't talk regularly, if I needed a place to stay that isn't home I know they would let me stay with them to feel safe. | | My therapist—they have said I can increase from monthly to weekly sessions if I need to. | |
| People who might be able to offer support. | | | My pastor. I do not have a close relationship with them, but they could offer spiritual support. | My old speech coach. I haven't talked to them in a while, but I always felt safe with them, and I know they volunteer at the women's shelter. |

Work and Hobbies

Work: Having to return to work reminds us that even though our lives are forever changed, the world is continuing to move forward. This can be incredibly overwhelming, especially if you haven't talked to your supervisor or human resources department about what you are experiencing. For some, it might not be a safe environment to discuss the situation at all. If you're working with a mental health team, consider asking them for medical accommodation notes to help excuse time off as needed. You may also want to find out if your employer offers employee assistance programs, which are nationwide programs that give employees a few free therapy sessions.

Hobbies: Consider making a list of the things you enjoyed doing before the assault and see how you can continue to do them, even if on a smaller scale. The familiarity can be comforting and help you to feel a sense of self again, and it may provide a moment of feeling "back to normal." If this sounds like it might be upsetting, set it aside for now. You can always pick up the hobby again later. For now, consider starting a different hobby, trying a new game, or learning a new skill. I picked up knitting after my assault as I was preparing to go to court, because I wanted something I could do with my hands. It took a lot of concentration at first, and eventually it became relaxing. I didn't expect for this new hobby to have such a positive impact on my healing and relationship with myself, but it did. You might also find simple pleasure in things you enjoyed when you were young, like coloring, finger painting, or playing with modeling clay.

LET'S CHECK IN

When you think about the skills, practices, or techniques that have been helpful to you in your self-care routines in the past, what comes to mind?

Start a list of the tools that have been effective and add to it when you discover new things that are helpful.

Looking ahead into Part II, we will cover strategies for disclosing our assault to those who will be supporting us (formally and informally). Reporting the crime is covered in greater detail. Much of the information we covered in Part I, such as sexual assault myths, understanding our trauma responses, identifying our support network, and grounding techniques, will help us moving forward. I know this is a lot to take in; take care of yourself first, and I will see you in Part II when you're ready.

Part II

CHAPTER 5

Deciding Who to Tell and What to Tell Them

In my experience, and in the experience of many survivors, the first time we hear ourselves say, "I was assaulted," the trauma somehow becomes even more real. When you decide you're ready to tell people you were assaulted—whether it just happened, it's been years, or decades—it won't be easy. And unfortunately, weighing the decision of whether or not to disclose and experiencing the weight of it doesn't end with the first person we tell. As you develop new relationships and enter into new situations, you will revisit these questions time and again. Do you tell your new significant other? Do you tell someone before you're intimate with them? Should you tell someone if they just disclosed their own assault to you? I can't make these decisions any easier, but I can help you to make them with greater confidence.

WHY DISCLOSURE CAN BE CHALLENGING

Many, many barriers exist that stop survivors from disclosing their assault. Some survivors, due to their culture, religion, or beliefs, think their value has changed after being assaulted and fear that their loved ones will view them differently if they disclose the assault. Others don't want to talk about the assault because revisiting the trauma can be incredibly and painfully triggering. Sometimes survivors repress memories about their assault, and there may be gaps in their recollection, so they may not feel confident disclosing. Some survivors either prefer to keep their experience to themselves or don't think they have anyone they can safely tell. You may be in any one of these situations, and ultimately the decisions are up to you. The most important part of disclosure is that you get to decide who to tell, and how. This is one of the things you can control.

Here are some reasons you may choose not to disclose your assault right away.

- You're experiencing self-blame or shame due to sexual assault myths (revisit the myths in chapter one).
- You don't think you will be believed.
- You don't want people talking about you or sharing the information with others.
- Cultural stigmas have made you feel like you won't be supported.
- You're afraid your significant other won't believe you or will say you're a cheater.
- You're concerned that people will question your sexuality.
- You're afraid of retaliation.

The Benefits of Disclosure

As difficult as disclosing can be, it can also be helpful. Shouldering this burden alone is exhausting. It's okay to ask for help; it's okay to share those dark thoughts, feelings, and fears with someone you trust, who can help lighten the burden.

Disclosing can also be an important part of building a support circle, people who will help you navigate next steps and think through important decisions—we talked about how important your support network is in chapter four. And, while it can be triggering, disclosing can also be an important step in acknowledging the trauma you experienced so you can begin your healing journey and decide what type of justice you may want to seek.

Some choose to disclose to help protect others in their community from the perpetrator. For example, someone may tell their employer that they were sexually assaulted by a coworker, not because they want to report the assault, but because they want to feel safer at work and want their coworkers to be safer, too. Or a college student may choose to disclose that they were harassed by a professor to make sure other students don't have to experience that unhealthy power dynamic or be harmed. There are also children who were assaulted by family members who don't disclose the assault until they're adults and have their own children who might be at risk from a cousin or other relative.

Protecting coworkers, other students, and family members are all brave and honorable choices. Remember, though, as a trauma survivor your own healing should be the highest priority, and you never need to disclose until you're ready.

You deserve to be heard.
You deserve to be believed.
You deserve to be supported.

Who Do I Tell?

You may feel like there are people you *should* tell—even so, nobody is entitled to your story. Instead of considering people you think you should disclose to, start with people you feel safe and comfortable with. Take into consideration how they've responded to stressful events in the past and what you might have heard them say or express about sexual assault cases or stories. Were they supportive of the survivor? Did they make victim-blaming comments? Do they understand what consent means? The person you want to tell first might be in your close personal circle, but sometimes it's easier and emotionally safer to tell a professional or a trusted community leader first.

Reasons to consider telling a professional first. A therapist, social worker, law officer, advocate, or spiritual leader can help you:

- process your feelings,
- access resources,
- decide who else to tell and how you want to tell them.

A mandated reporter is a professional who's legally required to report sexual assault to law enforcement if the person who discloses or reports assault or abuse is a minor or vulnerable adult. They don't want to violate your trust or get you in trouble; their role is to protect people from harm. If you want to make sure you don't unknowingly disclose to a mandated reporter, ask them if they are a mandated reporter before you disclose. In the report, the mandated reporter will include the victim survivor's name, age, contact information, the guardian's contact information, the name of the perpetrator (if known), and any information that was shared or witnessed that led the reporter to believe that abuse or assault occurred. They will report the abuse or assault to law enforcement or human services. After the report is made, human services and/or law enforcement will screen the report to see if it meets the criteria to follow up and investigate.

Examples of Mandated Reporters:
- teachers,
- health care professionals,
- social workers,
- daycare providers,
- psychologists and therapists,
- clergy members,
- law enforcement officers.

Telling people you trust. Ideally, your close friends and loved ones will respond in a supportive way, but sometimes initial responses can be less than ideal. Victims who have a negative experience when they disclose often find it harder to disclose again. It can help to remember that if someone responds negatively, it's not about you. It's typically about their emotions and/or lack of knowledge.

People you might choose to tell:

- close friend,
- family member with whom you have a safe relationship,
- supportive significant other,
- community or spiritual leader,
- teacher,
- sexual assault advocate or crisis line worker.

PREPARING TO DISCLOSE

Because preparing to share your experience can evoke many challenging emotions and concerns, it's helpful to plan ahead and check in with your body and mind before you have the conversation.

- Check in with your body and practice some grounding techniques (revisit chapter four).
- Make sure you feel like you're in a physically safe place.
- Remember you're in charge of all aspects of disclosing and can change course at any moment.
- Since you're in control, you can establish boundaries when you begin the conversation.
- Remember that this is about *you*, not *them*, so you get to decide how much you want to share, what questions, if any, you want to answer, and everything else about this conversation.
- If you start to feel triggered or overwhelmed, practice one of the grounding and coping techniques you learned in chapter four.

When to Disclose?

There is no *best time* to tell someone about your sexual assault. You may even be surprised by when you feel ready to tell someone, so it can help to prepare for that conversation ahead of time by deciding what you feel comfortable sharing and what boundaries you might want to put in place. For example, you might be having a casual conversation with someone when you realize you want to tell them, even though you hadn't planned on it. Knowing which boundaries you want in place for the conversation and what you're going to say to put the boundaries in place can help you feel more confident.

If you want to be very prepared, pick a day and time when you'll feel as safe as possible and can be as in control of the situation as possible. Also give some thought to what you might need after the talk. Do you want downtime in a quiet, cozy space where you can be surrounded by items that bring you comfort? Or do you want to go to a movie or do something active that provides a distraction? There are no right or wrong answers, so try to allow yourself to do whatever will help you to feel the safest.

What Do I Say?

Choosing to tell someone you were assaulted doesn't mean you have to share every detail. But trying to self-edit and decide what you feel safe sharing and what you want to keep to yourself while in the moment can be confusing, so it's helpful to make these choices before you have the conversation. It can also help to have some responses prepared in case they ask questions about details you don't want to share. You get to choose what parts of your trauma you share, and when. You do not owe anyone every detail of your story.

If the person you've confided in has follow-up questions, you might find that you don't know the answer. The brain has a powerful way of protecting itself, and you might not remember all the details. This is normal, and if that's the case, it's okay to say, "I don't know" or "I don't remember." You can also choose not to answer any follow-up questions, whether you recall the details clearly or not. See the following for sample scripts regarding disclosing your assault.

Sample Disclosure Scripts

Sometimes the things we need to say the most are the hardest to put into words. To help you frame what you want to say, I offer you some scripts for you to use or modify to fit your situation. To start the conversation, you might say:

- "I want to tell you about something that happened to me. I can really use your support right now."

- "I'm going through something that's hard for me to talk about."
- "There's something I need to share with someone, and I trust you."
- "Something happened to me that's very difficult for me to talk about, but I really need support."
- "I'm safe right now and it's not an emergency, but I'd like to share something with you that happened to me, and I can really use some support. Are you in an emotionally safe space to talk to me about it right now?" (This is more appropriate if time has passed between your assault and your disclosure to this person.)

During the conversation:

- "I'm not ready to talk about details, but I wanted to tell you I was sexually assaulted last night/week/year."

Or

- "I'm ready to share some additional details about what happened during my assault."

Setting boundaries, ending the conversation, and responding to questions:

- "I'm starting to feel overwhelmed and need a break. Can we come back to this later?"
- "I'm not ready to talk about that right now."
- "I'm not ready to talk about that. Thank you for respecting my boundaries."
- "I only feel comfortable sharing this part for now. Thank you for understanding."

- "Thank you for being here for me. I think I need a break right now."
- "I appreciate you being here for me. Right now, the best way you can support me is by: _____ (helping me access resources, helping me call law enforcement, staying with me while I try to ground myself, going with me to get ice cream and some fresh air)."

When Things Don't Go as Planned

No matter how well prepared you are to disclose your assault, you can't predict how someone will react. If they reassure you or offer you a hug, it can be very soothing. But if the person you're sharing with is shocked or upset by the news, they may not have a very helpful reaction. And if the person you tell has an extremely negative reaction, you may feel like you need to reassure or soothe *them*. Another barrier victims encounter is being interrupted or bombarded with questions. So, when you think about whether you want to share in person, consider whether you're ready for these possibilities.

Sometimes, even the people who love you don't know how to react. You may envision your friends or family members responding with sympathy, concern, and support, but instead:

- They share the time something similar or traumatic happened to them.
- They ask victim-blaming questions, like "Were you drinking?" or "What were you wearing?" and "How did you end up in this situation anyway?"
- They minimize your sexual assault and act like it wasn't a big deal.

Some examples of victim-blaming questions are:

- "What were you wearing?"
- "Isn't that the person you were dating a few weeks back?"
- "Was it your idea to go to their house?"
- "Was this before or after you started drinking?"
- "What did you do to stop them?"
- "Did you get an erection/were you aroused?"

These questions shift the blame from the perpetrator, where it belongs, to the victim. Sometimes these questions are intentionally asked to try to shame the victim, but more often they're subtle. The person asking these questions may not even realize they shift the blame or place shame on the victim, and these types of questions are often asked by people who either believe sexual assault myths or else they have not been educated about the realities of sexual assault.

The impacts of victim-blaming questions are dangerous. If survivors don't feel supported and assume the blame themselves, they're less likely to seek out the resources they need and less likely to report the crime. In addition to delaying the healing process, these questions also promote a culture in which perpetrators are not held accountable.

These types of reactions are somewhat common because they come from a place of shock (reacting without thinking) and ignorance (not knowing the best way to act), so being ready for this type of response can prevent you from being stunned or disappointed. Being ready for a negative reaction can also help you to be more prepared to point out how you're feeling, steer the conversation back to your story, and assertively stop any victim-blaming questioning. Try to be calm but firm about what you decided to share, keeping the boundaries you established.

Disclosing your story is not an easy step—but it is another one in your healing journey that will ultimately lead you to regain your sense of control.

EXPERT CONTRIBUTION: DISCLOSING SEXUAL ASSAULT
Sarah Mathews, MA, LMFT

Disclosing a traumatic experience(s) can be vulnerable and also empowering depending on the circumstances and where you are on your healing journey. The words you use to describe the experience(s), the aspects of the experience(s) that you share, and who you share the experience(s) with is your decision. Before deciding to disclose, it may be helpful to consider the following:

- What is my relationship with this person/how much do I trust this person?
- Is disclosing likely to be helpful, healing, and/or supportive?
- Am I emotionally/psychologically ready to talk about my experience, and to what degree?
- Are there any boundaries I would like to set or ask for?

Some people may not respond in a way that is helpful even if they are trying their best. Sometimes it can be difficult to start a conversation with someone you do trust. And sometimes it can be confusing to know what to do if the conversation heads in a direction that is uncomfortable or becomes hurtful. Here are some examples of words and phrases that you can use if you would like to disclose your experience(s) or would like to set a boundary:

- I would like to tell you about my traumatic experience(s) that may impact _____ (what—our relationship, this medical procedure, this sexual experience, etc.). Can I share that with you _____ (when—now, tomorrow, etc.) through _____ (method—writing, text, over dinner, etc.)?
- After I tell you about my experience(s), it would be helpful if you responded by _____ (action—holding my hand, not responding, etc.) after I've shared. Would that be okay for you?
- I would like to stop talking about this right now because I am feeling _____ (emotions—triggered, sad, uncomfortable, etc.). Can we _____ (action—take a break, walk, etc.)?
- I am not okay with how you are talking to me/responding to what I've shared. I am going to _____ (action—end conversation, leave, etc.) now.

You may feel more comfortable coming up with a plan ahead of time or saying something on the spot, and either is okay. It may also be helpful to plan some self-soothing techniques or supportive activities after disclosing (this can be solo or with the person with whom you shared). It can also be helpful to talk to a mental health professional beforehand and/or afterward to help you process and come up with a plan that feels right for you.

HOW TO RESPOND WHEN SOMEONE DISCLOSES SEXUAL ASSAULT

If you've been reading this book for yourself, you may want to share this section with someone you trust—it might help them when/if you're ready to disclose. This is also good advice for you—perhaps your disclosure may lead them to share details of their experience with you.

Learning that someone you care about has been the victim of a violent crime can evoke a wide range of emotions. You might feel angry, scared, useless, and even triggered if you're a victim of violence as well. All these emotions can make responding in a supportive way harder than you might expect. We all like to think that we'll handle difficult times with clarity and perfection, but we're all human. If someone has already disclosed to you and you're realizing that you didn't respond the way you would now that you know more about sexual assault, it's not too late to tell them that you're ready to be a strong support for them. Educating yourself, apologizing sincerely, and working to support them moving forward will go a long way.

If someone discloses to you:

- Listen, believe them, and tell them you believe them.
- Thank them for sharing this with you. It takes a lot of bravery and shows that they trust you. It is important to acknowledge this.
- No matter what emotions you're experiencing, it's important to allow the person who's disclosing to control the conversation.
- Avoid crossing your arms, turning away from the person, and other body language that can make it look like you don't believe them or you're not giving them your full attention. If known, it is important to consider what body language is in line with their culture as well.
- Don't touch or hug them without asking for permission.
- Reassure them by telling them this was not their fault.
- Remind them that their value has not been altered and that you will continue to be there for them.
- Don't make promises that you can't keep, like guaranteeing them that they'll get legal justice.

- Ask how you can best support them. Sometimes open-ended questions may be overwhelming, and it can help to offer options. For example, ask if they want to see a professional, talk to law enforcement, or go on a walk.
- Assure them that what happens next is up to them, and they can change their mind.
- Offer to go with them if they want to report the assault, but do not push them to report if they're not ready.
- Whether or not they think they want to report the crime, ask if they want help with preserving evidence or if they want you to go with them to see a medical professional.
- Check in with them frequently, but try not to hover, unless that's what they request.
- Keep checking in and inviting them to activities, events, and to spend time together. They may turn down the offers for a while, but knowing that you're thinking of them and wanting to include them is beneficial.

Michelle's Story

As a survivor, in the days after the attack I was lost and confused, but as each day passed, being raised to pray, I just prayed. I never got to share with my mother what happened, as she was mad at me because I came home late from school the evening of the rape. I had to return to school in Brooklyn, and every day I was afraid I would see him, but by the grace of God, I never did. I did not know what the future would hold, but always thanked God I survived. I never told anyone at school; I guess I felt if I told someone, they would spread the information around the school, and that would cause more embarrassment for me, so this became my own internal secret. After the attack, I wondered if he destroyed my insides. *Would I be able to get pregnant?* So many unanswered questions. Today, I can say that I have been blessed with four children and have become a wife, mom, grandmother, and even a great-grandmother. I did not know what the future would hold, but being raised to pray is what kept me going.

After my attack, I did not have a chance to quit or give up on life. When I was fourteen years old, my mother moved my baby brother into my room, and I became his caregiver. So, the evening of the rape, when my mother left for her class at the local college, I showered and cared for my brother. I was a sophomore in high school. There was no quitting because in reality I was caring for my brother full-time and I was a student. I could not quit because he needed me. I still had to return to my school, which was in Brooklyn, and the boy that assaulted me attended the school across the street. Did I share with anyone what happened? No, but my faith allowed me to pray and believe that I would be protected from my attacker.

In my younger years, I did not know what my purpose in life was, but as I continued to grow up, it became evident it was to help someone else know they too will recover and survive. Years later I was raped again, and my fight to help others became even stronger. I asked God to deliver me from that situation and became an advocate for women, sharing my testimony anywhere I go.

My healing came from my faith in God. I was raised by my great-grandmother, who taught me to pray. When she passed, my grandmother reminded me to always pray, knowing that God was always listening. When I came face-to-face with my attacker years later, I was eighteen years old and a mom to my own son. He was in a car with a young man I went to elementary school with. He was sitting in the back seat and said, "I know that b—h, I raped her." And when I saw his face, I immediately ran to my boyfriend's mom's house. At this stage in my life, I had to face the reality that the assault did happen, and I told my boyfriend's mother. She said, "You must tell him (my boyfriend) what happened to you." Now I had to tell my boyfriend, the father of my son and of all my future children, and I was so scared. When I began to share with him, he then shared that his sister was raped and never told anyone, and years later the same guy raped her again. Thank God I was not raped again by my attacker, and this is when, little by little, I was able to share my story of survival.

The words I use to encourage others is to never give up. We can use the trials and tribulations we face in our lives to help others. As we go through life, we never think that "rape" is something that will happen to us. After the assault, we ask ourselves many questions. What do I do? Do I tell someone? Will I get pregnant? Will others look at me differently? Should I report the rape? But as time goes on, we are able to change the statements we tell ourselves to "I was violated in the worst way, but survived."

It is okay to seek counseling for yourself. It will help in the healing process. It is okay to go to a support group and hear others' stories. The first few times you may not feel able to share, but one day, and most times it will be when you least expect it, you will hear your own voice sharing your story and how you too survived.

Love,

Michelle Davenport, DNP-RN

LET'S CHECK IN

Healing from trauma requires a lot of action, but it also requires rest. Before reading the next chapter, choose one action step and one resting activity and do them today.

Action Steps:
- Call a hotline and request local resources.
- Begin to write a plan to disclose your assault to someone.
- Use a search engine to find trauma therapists in your area.

Resting Steps:
- Choose a comfort movie to watch with hot chocolate and a warm blanket.
- Use your creativity to write a story, draw, paint, or make something.
- Go on a walk and stop to appreciate the flowers that you see along the way.

Recovery requires balance. Take the time you need today to invest in yourself and your healing journey.

CHAPTER 6

Your Support Team

Navigating life after trauma may feel isolating at times. Nobody can totally understand what you experienced, but some *will* understand enough to be helpful, and others will be able to offer support that's helpful in other ways. It isn't for me to say that it's impossible for you to begin healing your trauma without support, but I do know that you don't need to shoulder this alone, and everyone can benefit from a little help.

When you're processing a trauma, your mind is in survival mode, making it easy to miss areas of healing that are important to consider. I was so focused on returning to work and school that I didn't take into consideration what physical areas of healing I needed to address. Supportive services and people can help you to identify what you need in order to be safe and healthy. They can also help us process the trauma, pursue justice, access resources, and on the dark days they help us remember why we keep fighting.

There are formal and informal types of support. A **formal support** is a trained, hired/assigned professional, and is typically paid. These are therapists, social workers, advocates, and medical professionals. They can each support you in a variety of ways. For example, your primary care doctor will also make referrals to mental health services and help provide education around how trauma impacts the body. A therapist will offer resources that may be helpful in addition to providing therapy.

Informal supports are in your community and include your social network. These are family, friends, classmates, and other people you enjoy interacting with, like someone in your yoga class or someone you volunteer with.

CHOOSING YOUR PHYSICAL HEALTH SUPPORT TEAM

It's important to evaluate and address your physical health immediately after a sexual assault, due to the risks of pregnancy, sexually transmitted infections, and injuries. It's also important to address the long-term effects of trauma.

Primary care provider (PCP). A primary care provider is an essential part of your health care team because they provide medical care and help you to access other health care services. They may order medications, make referrals, and make sure your health care needs are met. In addition, they provide education around medical needs, lifestyle choices, and preventative care. A primary care provider can be a medical doctor, a doctor of osteopathic medicine, a nurse practitioner, clinical nurse specialist, or a physician assistant.

Massage therapist/acupuncturist/chiropractor. Being in a constant state of hypervigilance or tension related to PTSD makes muscles tight, and getting support to release that tension can help you to relax and even sleep better.

Some survivors find benefits in alternative therapies like massage, chiropractic adjustments, and acupuncture. These services, when provided by a practitioner who is trauma informed, can provide relaxation, help with PTSD symptoms, and increase positive awareness of our bodies.[18,19]

Physical and occupational therapist. Sexual violence can sometimes affect your body in ways that aren't easy to heal on your own. A physical therapist will support you by using exercises, stretches, and physical activities to improve movement, mobility, or function. Occupational therapists focus on helping you to improve motor skills so you can perform daily tasks with more ease, and they can also make recommendations for how to modify your home or work environment so you can be more physically functional. Another treatment to consider is pelvic floor physical therapy. Survivors of sexual assault are more likely to have pelvic floor dysfunction than people who have not been assaulted.[20] Symptoms of pelvic floor dysfunction can include constipation; lower back pain; pain in the pelvis, rectum, and genitals; painful intercourse; and feeling the frequent need to urinate.

Nutritionist and dietitian. Trauma survivors sometimes use food as a way to cope, so having support can help you to continue to have a healthy relationship with food and to heal eating disorders whether they're old or new. It's not uncommon for people with eating disorders to have a history of sexual abuse.[21] Nutritionists and dietitians help you evaluate your eating habits and diet, set nutrition goals, and create a nutritional plan.

Not all states require nutritionists to have certifications, but all states require dietitians to be registered. (Becoming registered includes receiving a degree from an approved program, completing some supervised program such as an internship, and passing a national examination.) If you have a history of eating disorders or think you might be developing one, your primary care provider will most likely recommend that you see a dietitian.

Fitness programs. It's not unusual for sexual assault survivors to feel a lack of power over their bodies. Intentionally moving your body can remind you that it is *your* body. It can also be a safe way to release emotions. If you don't have a favorite way to move your body, explore until you find something that feels good to you. Some survivors swear by running; others say yoga is a lifesaver for them. Some survivors find quiet hikes healing, others like competitive sports, some like group classes, and some prefer being with just one friend or a fitness coach. If you feel safer at home, there are all kinds of online courses you can try, and some of them are free or offer free trials.

EXPERT CONTRIBUTION: Q & A WITH A DIETITIAN
Angela Goens, MS, RDN, LD

How can a dietitian support those who have experienced trauma?

A registered dietitian (RD) or registered dietitian nutritionist (RDN) can be very supportive for individuals who have experienced trauma. Please be sure to screen your RDN and ask questions about their trauma training before beginning to work together. Working with someone who is not properly trained could create more harm for a new client. Traditional training and education for dietitians does not include more than basic 101 counseling and psychology classes. However, there are many registered dietitians who have advanced training and education, often coupled with life experience, that make them qualified to provide trauma-informed nutrition support. It will also be important to find a provider who understands the systemic barriers for those struggling with mental illness and trauma.

Dietitians use a thoughtful, individualized, person-centered approach for treatment. The intention is to avoid blaming and shaming a client because our world can often be so phobic, fearful, stigmatizing, and judgmental. We collaborate with clients to understand what nutrition goals seem realistic to achieve and maintain. This often means meeting someone where they are in that moment or helping them in the short term. If a client has just recently gone through a traumatic event, their goals are often different than those of survivors who are years post-trauma, so RDNs customize plans for each client, being flexible with education, meal planning, movement, and body image support.

What role does nutrition play in managing or exacerbating symptoms of PTSD, depression, or other mental health diagnoses?

Nutrition can play an important role in enhancing a person's overall mental health and well-being. Nutritional support with the right balance of nutrients and adequate amounts of food will provide energy and can improve mood. If a person is undernourished, they can't properly absorb medications, so drugs might not work as effectively as they were intended. In addition to nutrition, a dietitian can also provide recovery support that includes movement, sleep, and hydration.

If food was involved in a negative experience or traumatic event, it can be particularly helpful to work with a skilled RD who understands the complexities of trauma and can assess the whole picture, including the client's history with food. This must be carefully done to avoid further traumatizing an individual, while simultaneously finding ways to empower and encourage clients to choose food that will nourish their brain and body.

Have you noticed any connections between eating disorders and trauma?

Eating disorders and trauma are both very complex, but a common thread between them is feeling disconnected from one's body. The dissociation that is often a result of trauma can lead to a strong lack of awareness of basic needs. This can look like minimal self-care, extreme behaviors with food (for example, bingeing), avoidance of hunger by restricting, mistrust of body cues, compensatory behaviors, weight fluctuations, body shaming, self-harm, and many other behaviors.

An eating disorder can be a coping mechanism for those who have experienced trauma. This adaptive form of coping becomes a way of survival for some. In fact, manipulating food, behaviors or rituals with food, and rigid rules can give a person a sense of control and safety back in their life. In order to begin rebuilding a relationship with self and one's body after a traumatic event, it is very important for support people, like dietitians, to understand the controlling of food is not actually much about food at all. There are also other impactful components of an individual that can contribute to eating disorders and are important to assess beyond food, such as identity, gender expression, race, financial status, and other socioeconomic factors. Consider seeking support from a trauma-informed dietitian if you might need guidance with nourishing yourself after a traumatic event and/or disordered eating patterns.

What is one practice that can help us to have a better relationship with food?

Most people would agree that food is meant to provide the body with energy. However, it's important to remember that food has many other purposes, including being comforting, soothing, distractive, joyful, pleasurable, satisfying. So it's not surprising that it's sometimes used to cope with intense stressors.

To help people get a better understanding of the way food affects them, I provide basic nutrition education and share how taking care of the digestive system/gut can directly help the brain, thus impacting mental health. For many clients, a helpful daily practice to prompt a more connected relationship with food is removing judgment. This means for yourself and others! Some examples might be eating dessert daily, eating convenience foods to save time, eating out because you don't like to cook or never learned how, eating meals that don't look like social media posts, or eating whatever is available at the food shelf because that's your primary food source; it all needs no judgment. Rigid food rules have no place in a mended, flexible, and kind relationship with food.

For someone who's experiencing an eating disorder after trauma, what are some steps to rebuild their relationship with food?

First, it's important to understand that addressing an eating disorder in the aftermath of a trauma can be particularly challenging, because this can be a difficult time to rebuild trust with food and with your body. Find a skilled trauma-informed registered and licensed dietitian to help you to unpack current behaviors with food. Ideally, they will be an identity-affirming, weight inclusive, and culturally competent RD who can support recovery and minimize additional harm in the process.

A dietitian can be a crucial part of your interdisciplinary mental health team. Explore with an RD why certain behaviors manifest themselves via particular food patterns. These sessions can be helpful to improve overall mental health and well-being. There are many skilled RDs who understand the complexities of trauma. Here are a few places to find clinicians who specialize in eating disorders and trauma-informed medical nutrition therapy:

National Alliance for Eating Disorders Awareness (www.alliance foreatingdisorders.com)

Project HEAL (www.theprojectheal.org)

FEDUP (fedupcollective.org)

SUPPORT FROM SURVIVORS: SOURCES OF UNEXPECTED SUPPORT

Support doesn't always come from where we most expect it, or from whom we most expect it. Survivors share people and places where they found understanding, validation, strength, and support.

"My personal trainer."

"A fellow AA member."

"My communications class professor."

"My yoga instructor."

"My coworker."

"The nurses at the inpatient unit I went to."

"The fictional characters I met while reading fantasy books."

"The women's center on my college campus."

"The psychiatrist who became my biggest cheerleader and advocate."

"I started going dancing, and although they didn't know it, the friendly and caring people who went to that dance class with me made a huge impact."

"The director of my play made sure to always support me."

"A longtime best friend who made a point to check in on me."

"My mother-in-law became a go-to person for me."

"Another person who was in the inpatient hospital with me."

"I started to travel a few years ago. It was terrifying at first, but I have met so many strangers who have touched my life forever."

CHOOSING YOUR MENTAL HEALTH SUPPORT TEAM

The impact that sexual assault has on our mental health can go ignored, since injuries to our mental health can seem invisible compared to the physical injuries that we can see. A key component to addressing the effect trauma has on our mental health is to build mental health professionals into our care team early in our healing process (see chapter eleven for a more in-depth discussion about the impacts of trauma on mental health).

Therapist. Therapists are licensed and might work in an office, hospital, treatment center, or private practice. They support your mental and emotional health, including behavioral patterns and addictions. Some therapists focus on specific styles of therapy such as cognitive behavioral (CBT), animal assisted, dialectal behavioral (DBT), or eye movement desensitization reprocessing (EMDR). These therapies are described in chapter twelve. A therapist can't prescribe medications, but they can refer you to other treatment options, including psychiatrists, who are authorized to prescribe medications.

Psychiatrist. A psychiatrist is a medical doctor who can prescribe medication and monitor the effectiveness of the medications and the potential side effects. Psychiatrists can make diagnoses and can evaluate both the physical and the mental aspects of a diagnosis.

You might be reluctant to get an official mental health diagnosis, but know that it can help open doors to more services and support, and this documentation is necessary to apply for financial aid, disability status for work, or Social Security disability benefits.

Psychologist. Psychologists have studied human behavior and mental processes and how people interact with their environment. They do many of the same things as psychiatrists, but they're not medical doctors and can't prescribe medications. A clinical psychologist has a doctorate in psychology and can diagnose and create a treatment plan for mental health and developmental disorders.

Social worker. A social worker connects you to resources such as financial and legal resources in your community and helps you to address other needs like meals, transportation, and support groups. Social workers may work in a hospital, government, educational, advocacy, or independent setting. Child Protective Services is an example of a social work agency. Other social work agencies provide personal care assistance, employment support, and disability services. Depending on the agency, you may need to qualify for a social worker based on requirements such as income limits or disability status. It never hurts to advocate for yourself and ask if social workers are available to you.

Support groups. Support groups can be incredibly beneficial for survivors of sexual assault. They provide a safe environment to share your experiences and to receive and offer support. These are led by a professional to make sure the conversation stays safe and respectful.

Therapists, psychologists, psychiatrists, social workers, and advocacy agencies can all tell you where to find support groups, and help you find ones that are led by qualified individuals. You can also find these groups online by using the keywords "support group," "sexual assault survivor," "PTSD," "anxiety," and your geographic location. Know that you can leave any support groups that make you uncomfortable or do not feel appropriate for you.

Social media platforms. Social media platforms may not be the top of your list when you think of support, but many survivors find them very helpful as a starting place to get information regarding sexual assault. These platforms can provide education and validation when all other options seem inaccessible or if there are barriers to receiving other services. A benefit of social media platforms is the access you have to large communities of survivors all over the world. If you live in a small town with few resources, you can follow a large platform in another location for information and support. If the information is overwhelming, be sure to take social media breaks (you can change your notification settings, put your phone on do not disturb mode, or decide to not look at social media during certain hours if needed) to control when you receive information about potentially triggering topics. Not all social media sites have accurate or up-to-date information, so it is important to vet your sources and do your own research to confirm what you read. For example, you may find a post that says the statute of limitations in your state is three years, which means you cannot report your assault, but after doing more research find out that since that post was shared your state has changed that statute and you now have an opportunity to report.

Other people to consider. You can improve your mental health in many different ways. For example, you might find support and sense of community in fitness classes, feel a sense of accomplishment from learning more about a subject you enjoy, or receive helpful advice from an instructor. One of the biggest breakthrough moments on my own healing journey occurred when I was taking advanced horseback-riding lessons. I had been riding, training, and showing horses for ten years, and on this particular summer day, I was riding Mungo, a high-energy black stallion. This horse was new to me, and I knew I needed to give my full attention to riding, but my mind kept wandering, so Mungo was wandering all over the arena, too. I was embarrassed and frustrated that I couldn't even get him to walk in a straight line. My instructor, who could be intimidating, told me to stop and look at him. As I held back tears, he said in his thick Austrian accent, "Remember to ride the same way you should do anything in your life, with intention." And then he smiled, which he rarely did, and even gave me a friendly wink of encouragement before telling me to try again. That one piece of advice helped Mungo and me to work better together, but what was more significant is that it made me think about how I could add intention into my healing journey. And my instructor's kindness in a moment when I felt defeated reminded me to keep going and keep trying.

Any interest you feel drawn to can provide an environment for healing and self-rediscovery. Survivors have found mental health benefits in theater programs, where they gained confidence about pursuing their dreams and also found an accepting community where they could safely express themselves. Other survivors find healing in dancing, art therapy, writing, and other creative pursuits.

SUPPORT FROM SURVIVORS: ACTS OF KINDNESS ON SURVIVORS' HEALING JOURNEYS

Sometimes acts of kindness are spontaneous, and some are planned. Here are some examples of kindness impacting survivors of sexual violence.

"A person who had been supporting me in the beginning part of my journey saw me after some time had gone by and said that they could tell I was further along on my healing journey, I looked like I felt lighter. I remember being moved that they remembered me at all, and then I also felt hope that I was healing and growing even if I didn't see it in the moment."

"A professor offered to sit with me in silence so I wasn't alone, even without me having to share the details. She knew that I just needed someone to be there with me."

"My best friend gave me a card saying that it took strength to go through what I was, but that I didn't need to be strong all the time and that she would be there for me every step of the way."

"Someone offered to go with me to the women's center when I was experiencing doubt and confusion about if I had actually been raped. The person coming with me supported me just by offering to go with me, and then the advocate at the shelter showed so much kindness in explaining to me what rape was and what rape myths looked like."

"Some coworkers at work heard what happened to me, and they told me that we were all family, and they walked with me to my car to help me feel safe."

"Someone encouraged and pushed me to go to therapy. I didn't want to, but I am glad that I listened."

"My mother reached out to me and reminded me to eat food and even brought me my favorite snacks without me needing to ask. I never expected her to show up for me in that way."

LET'S CHECK IN

Reaching out for help can be hard. Asking for help can make us feel vulnerable, and after a trauma, that can be really scary. Now that you've given some thought to the types of physical and mental health care support that you want, take some time to think about other people who might offer support that you'll appreciate. Revisit the relationship map in chapter four and fill in more supports or providers who will be helpful to you as you move forward. And remember to think outside of the box. Your support team and healing plan will be as unique as you.

CHAPTER 7

Seeking Justice

In a perfect world, reporting our sexual assault would lead to our feeling a sense of justice. In reality, reporting and testifying can be a re-traumatizing process, so it's normal to have questions about the hows and whys of reporting.

First, it's important to know that while reporting your assault may not lead to the outcome you're seeking, some survivors still find doing so helpful because it allows them to hold their perpetrators accountable. Other survivors have said they don't feel like reporting was a necessary part of their healing process. Even if you don't want to report, understanding the reporting process can help you feel more confident in your decision. I waited three years before I reported being assaulted, and I was confused if it even was assault because I knew the person and I didn't fight back as hard as I thought I should have. When I learned that it was assault, it took a while to define what justice meant for me. Reporting didn't satisfy my need for justice, but it did give me the opportunity to do what I could to hold my perpetrator accountable.

IS REPORTING AN OPTION FOR ME?

Reporting might seem like it's only an option when the assault looked like what's commonly depicted in the media: a physically violent assault by a stranger in a dark alley. But we know how far this is from the reality of most sexual assault cases. (To review the commonly held sexual assault myths, refer to the section 12 Myths About Sexual Assault on page 14.)

You may be asking yourself if you can report if:

"I know my perpetrator."
"I was drinking that night."
"It was weeks ago. I don't think there's any evidence."
"I don't remember every detail."

The answer is yes, you can still report your assault. There are also other options to consider for seeking justice outside of criminal court, such as civil court, or Title IX. We'll review all these options in detail at the end of this chapter. Because the criminal court system is what most survivors of assault think of when they consider reporting, it's helpful to understand more about that process, so we'll begin there.

Statute of Limitations

Statutes of limitations are laws that specify how much time can pass between when a crime is committed and when law enforcement can act on the report or the state can move forward with charges. These statutes vary by state, and the differences are based on factors like the current age of the victim, the age of the victim at the time of the crime, if there's DNA evidence available, and what degree of crime was committed (such as a felony versus a misdemeanor). These statutes can act as a barrier for survivors who didn't report immediately after the crime.

The good news is that advocates and activists around the country are pushing for policy changes to extend or eliminate these limitations. Because the statutes are always changing, the best way to research the ones in your state is through the RAINN.org website, which updates information on statutes of limitations regularly. You can also contact a victim advocate in your state and ask them for information regarding statutes. You can find an advocacy center by calling the National Sexual Assault Hotline at 1-800-656-4673.

Delayed Reporting

There are many reasons assault survivors don't report right after the crime. Trauma impacts both brain and body, and the immediate trauma post-assault may cause the victim to dissociate, feel disoriented, and be confused about what they just experienced. Sometimes survivors don't report because they're afraid of repercussions, feel they have a lack of support, or don't know they have the option to report. It's important for you to know that no matter how much time has passed, the statutes of limitations do not prevent you from reporting the crime. Some choose to make a report, even though they know the statute of limitations has expired, because it feels empowering. Another reason to consider reporting even if the time to take legal action has passed is that if the perpetrator commits sexual assault again and one of his victims files a report, your report can help to strengthen the other survivor's case.

During the #MeToo movement in 2017, people came forward with stories of assaults that had happened years earlier. This gave a voice to people who had felt silenced for years. Helping the general public, judges, and jurors to understand that it's common for sexual assault survivors to delay disclosing and reporting can result in more guilty verdicts in the future.

EXPERT CONTRIBUTION: DELAYED REPORTING
Detective Shelly Fisher

Contrary to the stereotypical film drama of the stranger who appears out of nowhere to commit sexual violence, in reality, that scenario is rare. Sexual assaults are generally committed by a known person, and the stronger the relationship is, the less likely a victim will disclose. Many were children when the assault or ongoing abuse occurred; some continued into or happened in adulthood. Regardless of the sexual violence taking place once or multiple times as a child or adult, the individuals often wait years to decades before disclosing, and the majority will keep this a secret their entire lives. This delay in reporting is the norm for children and adult victims of sexual violence.

It can be hard for others to comprehend why a victim didn't immediately report an act so intimate and violent as a sexual assault. The disclosure of sexual assault is not an event, but a process over time that is unique to everyone because of a multitude of factors. The decision to tell can be delayed for one or many reasons, including being in a state of paralyzing shock after the assault, fear of not being believed, not having a support system, threats, fear of the court process, fear of retaliation, guilt that they "let" this happen, and mistakenly believing it was their fault. These fears and uncertainties encourage victims to suffer in silence, causing psychological distress and delay of necessary medical care.

Most cases do not have any physical evidence. Physical evidence is helpful, but isn't required to successfully prosecute a sexual assault. Investigations can proceed if the statute of limitations hasn't expired, and those laws vary by state. I've had many conversations with victims reporting long after the statute of limitations has expired. It's heartbreaking to hear their stories and not be able to help them achieve justice.

When a victim decides to follow through with a criminal investigation from a delayed disclosure, the investigator will try to obtain as much information as possible to corroborate what happened. Even though it's a difficult process, victims typically experience some relief after disclosing in a safe place to an empathetic ear. The well-being of the victim is paramount to any criminal aspect of the investigation. What's important to us in law enforcement is that we treat each survivor with dignity and respect and honor the courage and strength it took to disclose the assault.

Many confidential community resources are available to survivors of sexual violence. I encourage survivors to seek out these resources as soon as you are ready, to help lessen the trauma, obtain medical treatment, and get assistance with any other needs.

DECIDING TO REPORT

Some survivors immediately know they want to report the crime, and some know they don't want to report it; either way, there's a lot to consider before you make a decision. When you're deciding if you want to report, it's helpful to know:

- You have rights as a victim of a crime.
- You're not obligated to report.
- You don't have to report right away, but reporting as soon as possible after the assault can strengthen your case and help you

access resources more quickly. (See chapters two and three for the benefits of reporting right away and how to save evidence.)

- You don't have to navigate this process alone. Victim advocates are beneficial resources to consider.
- Due to the effects of trauma, it's normal to have gaps in your memory. This may make you hesitant to report, but anything you share can be useful in the investigation. If you don't remember a detail, it's okay to say that you don't remember.
- In a criminal court case, you're not the one who is pressing charges. Once you make the report, law enforcement may ask if you want to move forward with charges, but the state will make the final decision. Typically, the victim's preferences are taken into consideration, but the state can move forward even if the survivor doesn't want to do so.
- Since you're not the one pressing charges in a criminal court case, you will not be responsible for any legal fees. This is different if you choose the civil court route. (See the Civil Court section on page 195.)
- It's impossible to guess or guarantee any specific outcome of reporting, but the option to report is something that's in your control.

Your Rights as a Victim

According to the United States Department of Justice, all victims of crime have the right to:

- be reasonably protected from the accused,
- reasonable and timely notice of court proceedings and to not be excluded from those proceedings,

- be heard at courtroom proceedings,
- communication with the attorney representing the government (the prosecuting attorney),
- restitution,
- timely proceedings,
- be informed of plea bargains,
- be informed of all these rights.[22]

Questions to ask yourself when you consider reporting:

- Do I have the support I need to report? If not, what can I do to get that support?
- How will reporting affect my mental well-being? If it will be too hard on me, should I wait?
- How will I feel if I report but no charges are made?
- Do I feel safe to make a report? If not, what will help me feel safer?
- What barriers do I have to reporting?
- How can reporting be helpful to me?

How Reporting Can Help

Because making the decision to report can feel intimidating, I want to share some reasons it's still worth considering. Reporting is a way to feel that you're taking back some control from the perpetrator of your assault. No matter how the investigation unfolds, you can hold the perpetrator accountable for their crime, and reporting may help to protect other people from the perpetrator.

Reporting can also help us to make lasting changes in awareness about sexual assault and the legal system. The available data shows how often and under what circumstances assaults occur. These statistics also show that the need for resources to support victims of assault dramatically exceeds the resources and support that is currently available.

SUPPORT FROM SURVIVORS: ENCOURAGEMENT AND ADVICE ABOUT REPORTING

No two people will have the same experience or story in regard to their trauma or their reporting process. A variety of survivors share their encouragement and advice around reporting.

"Go with what feels right to you, not what others expect you to do. Know your options; every decision is valid!"

"You deserve to have your story heard. Reporting can give you the space to share what happened to you."

"What happened to you wasn't your fault. Move forward in whatever way is most healing to you."

"I know you might feel very alone, but know thousands of sexual assault survivors have gone before you and paved the way for you to report. You can join them and help pave the way for future survivors."

"You can't control where the case goes. But you do have the power to try and do what you can to hold them accountable."

"You deserve this. To report. To be heard. No assault is too 'small' to deserve that."

"I wish I had acted sooner and reported earlier. I have learned to be kind to myself and know I made the best decision for me with the information and support I had at the time."

"You aren't weak or invalid for choosing not to report."

"Keep fighting. The fight will look different for everyone and
may or may not include reporting. But keep fighting."

"Look and gather all legal advice you can to make an
informed decision."

"I wish I had reported. I found out later he hurt someone else.
I know it wasn't my fault but I still feel bad."

"It is completely your choice, but please make sure you have
support and are prepared for how difficult it is, and be
ready to advocate for yourself."

" It is important that you take your best interest and healing
as the priority."

"Talk to a trusted friend or counselor before and set up a time
to talk to them after and debrief."

The Reporting Process

The reporting process is different in each city, depending on factors
including the resources that law enforcement has available. The information in this section is general, so be sure to connect with your local
resources for information specific to your state. As you prepare to
report, consider the following:

- If you're in immediate danger, call 911, and help will come to
  you.
- Make a list of your questions. For example, does the law enforcement agency have advocacy services they will provide? Who can
  you call if you remember more information? How long will it be
  before you receive follow-up information?

- Consider who you want to take with you for support.
- Have a conversation with a victim advocate in your state or use other resources such as RAINN to find out what the sexual assault laws are in your state.
- You can go to the local police department or make a report over the phone.
- If your assault happened on your college campus, you can contact the campus law enforcement center.
- If you go to a health care center for treatment or a forensic exam, you can make your report there.
- You can also visit a sexual assault advocacy center.

When you call or go to the police station to make a report, you will most likely speak with a patrol officer who will ask the who, what, where, and when questions, while also ensuring that your immediate safety needs are met and addressed. They will create a report with the information and determine how quickly they need to follow up on the report. They will ask if you still have contact with the perpetrator, if you have any fears about your safety, and if so, they'll create a safety plan with you.

When your initial report is reviewed, a detective will be assigned to gather information for a full report. The amount of time between when you make the initial report and when you hear from a detective can vary. Ask during your initial report what a realistic timeline is for a detective to reach out to you, and ask who to contact for follow-up if you don't hear from the detective within the given timeframe. After speaking with you, the detective will determine if there's enough information to proceed with an investigation. Please see page 150 for more information.

While you're reporting, you have a right to privacy and to be in a quiet space. Some questions may feel uncomfortable, and the officer may ask questions multiple times, which can make it seem like they don't believe or trust you. But because trauma can affect our ability to recall details, sometimes being asked a question in different ways or at different points in your account can help you to remember more details. The officers will ask you to be specific, including using anatomical terms for genitals and disclosing as many details as you can remember. It can be helpful to practice saying some of these words out loud beforehand if they make you feel triggered. After you complete your report, law enforcement may contact you again if they have follow-up questions or decide to open an investigation.

During the reporting process, you deserve to be treated with trauma-informed care, which includes feeling heard, being respected, and having all your questions and concerns addressed. If you don't feel you were given fair and respectful treatment, do not be afraid to go up the chain of command and report your concerns to the officer's supervisor. You also can share your concerns and complaints with victim advocates. If you feel you were not respected by law enforcement (or any professional supporting you), consider the following actions:

- Document everything, including dates, times, locations, names of individuals involved, and what was said or done.
- Consult with an attorney if you feel that your rights were not upheld.
- Seek support from your informal and formal support team.
- Work with advocates to get information about your options when you feel you were not respected.
- Speak to a manager or higher-level authority and share with them your concerns and what you have documented.
- Practice self-care and know that their lack of support shows lack of training and education on their part and is not a reflection on you.

Caring for Yourself Through the Reporting Process

The reporting process is unfamiliar and can be stressful. Knowing that there will be several unknowns can make taking this step feel daunting. Putting the crime in the hands of law enforcement can feel like you're relinquishing control because they take over the process and have the authority to open an investigation or choose not to. It's helpful to remember that reporting will actually help you to take back control by holding the perpetrator accountable for the crime.

Here are some other things you can do to help yourself as you navigate this process:

- Learn at least two grounding or coping techniques, like deep breathing and recalling positive affirmations, that you can use if you start to feel triggered.
- Keep a fidget toy or some sensory item you can touch or hold on to as needed.
- Know you can ask to take breaks if you begin to feel overwhelmed.
- Bring pen and paper so you can write down questions you have, as you have them.
- You can ask for a copy of your report.

SUPPORT FROM SURVIVORS: HOW VICTIM ADVOCATES SUPPORTED SURVIVORS DURING THE REPORTING PROCESS

Support can include many different things. Sometimes it's having someone share resources with you or directly advocating with the judicial or health care system on your behalf. Other times it's just knowing that someone you trust is in your corner. Survivors share ways that advocates have supported them during the reporting process.

"They gave me a sense of community, belonging, and
    solidarity."
"They helped me feel like a person throughout the process,
    not just a victim."
"She was the first to say 'I believe you' and actually listened."
"They helped me understand the process of all the legal stuff
    and answered my questions."
"She actually would get back to me with answers when I felt
    like no one else was responding to me."
"I felt like I had someone in this with me, who had some idea
    of how hard this was."

FALSE REPORTS: RARE BUT DAMAGING

False reports of sexual assault are extremely uncommon. Current data indicates a range of only 5 to 8 percent of reported sexual assaults are false.[23] When you consider that only 63 percent of sexual assaults are reported to law enforcement,[24] it's clear that false reports make up a fraction of the total number of reported assaults, but the damage they can do is significant. Two of the most common reasons survivors hesitate to report the crime is they don't know if they will be believed, and they don't know if their assault is "serious" enough to warrant authorities' attention.

The following are *not* false reports:

- When someone chooses not to report the assault right away, or at all.
- If law enforcement or the district attorney's office chooses not to move forward with the investigation.
- If law enforcement is not supportive or is disrespectful or unprofessional.
- If the victim does not get their day in court.
- If the perpetrator is not found guilty.

EXPERT CONTRIBUTION: VICTIM ADVOCATES AND REPORTING TO LAW ENFORCEMENT

Bree Theising-Stair, Sexual Violence Advocate

If a victim/survivor decides to report to law enforcement, they may want sexual violence advocacy support during those proceedings. Victims/survivors have the right to have an advocate present during the initial statement, investigative interview, and for any meetings or phone calls thereafter. Once the case has been investigated by law enforcement it is sent to the county attorney's office (county where the crime occurred). Then, the victim/survivor is assigned to a prosecutor and a victim witness advocate. *A victim witness advocate is different than a sexual violence advocate because they do not hold the same confidentiality.* In other words, this means anything stated to a victim witness advocate is shared with prosecution, whereas anything shared with a sexual violence advocate is confidential and not shared unless it's a mandated report. A victim/survivor may also request a sexual violence advocate to be present with them throughout the court process.

EXPERT CONTRIBUTION: TITLE IX:
A DEEP DIVE

Bree Theising-Stair, Sexual Violence Advocate

Title IX was enacted in 1972 stating: "No person in the United States shall, on the basis of sex, be excluded from the participation in, be denied the benefits of, or be subjected to discrimination under any education program or activity receiving Federal financial assistance." (Know Your IX, 2023)

Title IX holds educational institutions to a standard of evaluating and investigating any form of sexual harassment report, including sexual violence. The educational institutions must also implement policies and procedures to respond to these reports. These institutions receive federal funding that they can lose if accusations of Title IX violations are not properly investigated. Institutions must promptly take action on any report of sexual harassment and sexual violence to remain in compliance. If educational institutions are not in compliance, they will be investigated by the US Department of Education Office of Civil Rights and may lose some or all federal funding and/or be required to pay damages.

The Title IX statute also requires educational institutions to employ a Title IX coordinator to ensure students on the campus are safe, the institution maintains compliance with Title IX, and students and faculty are aware of Title IX rules and regulations. If you find your college or university doesn't have a Title IX coordinator, it's not in compliance with Title IX and should be reported.

Reporting Options for Title IX

Schools under Title IX are required to adopt and publish a grievance procedure outlining the steps of reporting violations to campus public safety and/or the Title IX coordinator. These grievance procedures must protect the victim/survivor from being asked anything about their sexual or medical histories. Victims/survivors have the right to report to campus and/or law enforcement in the jurisdiction of the crime (city/county). The report to the Title IX coordinator and/or any employee of the educational institution may also include accommodations to classes, activities, room/board, etc., and this is not solely on the victim/survivor, but working together to create a safer space. The initial report, if not made to the Title IX coordinator, will be shared under the policy of the institution. Under Title IX guidance, the accuser and accused have the same rights to information.

After a complaint of a Title IX violation, there is a pre-hearing, hearing, and appeal hearing. The information presented in the hearings is shared with both parties. The victim/survivor may have an adviser and/or attorney present for support and advocacy. During the hearing process, the standard of proof is high. The victim/survivor, with an adviser and/or attorney, must prove the preponderance of evidence. This means they must prove it is more likely (51 percent) than not that a crime occurred and warrants the finding of a Title IX violation.

OPTIONS BESIDES CRIMINAL COURT

Pursuing criminal court is not the only option that you have regarding holding your perpetrator accountable or seeking justice. Some other options are explored below.

Title IX

Title IX is a federal rights law that was passed in 1972 to protect people from discrimination based on sex in educational settings. As part of Title IX, educational institutions that receive federal funding are required to protect and provide security for their students, faculty, and staff from sexual discrimination or the college may be liable for damages and legal fees. Educational institutions are also required to put procedures in place for handling sexual violence and discrimination complaints, and those who report these violations can't be retaliated against.

Title IX is controversial—many survivors who were assaulted in educational settings say their education was interrupted or suffered and the school did not respond with a formal investigation.[25] The Know Your IX organization supports and advocates for survivors in educational settings and provides them with resources.

Civil Court

In civil court, you handle your case along with an attorney that you hire. Unlike in criminal court proceedings, the goal isn't to determine the guilt or innocence of the accused. The goal in a civil case is to determine if the defendant is liable for the damages you experienced. If the accused is found liable, they may have to compensate you for medical expenses, psychological damage, lost wages, and more. Someone who has been sexually assaulted can bring their case to civil court, even if the defendant was found not guilty in criminal court.

Civil court gives you more control over your case. You can hire your own attorney and will be more involved with gathering the evidence that will be presented.

It's possible to pursue both civil and criminal court options. To move forward, contact an attorney for more information. Attorney Ryan Krupp shares some advice on how to find an attorney in chapter nine.

Restorative Justice as an Alternative Form of Justice

The restorative justice process is gradually becoming an option for survivors of sexual assault to hold their perpetrator accountable without direct involvement of the legal and judicial system. At this time, it's most commonly used for minor crimes and crimes involving youth; more serious cases such as sexual assault are not typically recommended for the restorative justice process. However, some survivors are interested in this process and believe that they are given more of a voice. In restorative justice, the victim of the crime, the perpetrator, and members of the community are involved in a mediated process with trained facilitators that provides an opportunity for all parties involved to reflect on the aftermath of the crime and the harm caused while looking forward with a preventative and creative problem-solving mindset.[26] It can give the survivors a greater sense of agency, voice, and control over the process, but it is not appropriate for all cases and depends greatly on the willingness of all parties to engage in the process. In restorative justice, the focus is on emotional recovery and community healing/reintegration, rather than punitive outcomes. This is a developing option, and may not be available in all jurisdictions, and the process may differ in each jurisdiction. If you're interested in learning more about this, reach out to a sexual assault advocate and request more information.

Steven's Story

When something awful like this happens to you, it robs you of your agency; it truly diminishes your light and joy. After I was assaulted, it completely changed the trajectory of my life in ways I never could have imagined. Picking up the pieces after is never easy, but it is truly possible, and every single survivor deserves to have their light back. The truth is I didn't think I would be myself again. I like to say that part of myself "died" that day, but through it all I began to come back to life as a better and stronger person every single day. I sit here two years later writing this and looking back at myself and wanting to give that scared and unsure boy a big hug and tell him that we are gonna be okay. Healing takes time. When I was assaulted, I thought I could never trust anyone ever again. I was nineteen at the time, and people my age were in relationships and dating. I thought I could never do that after what happened to me because I just could not trust anyone.

I am twenty-one now and in the happiest, most healthy relationship with a man who I want in my life forever. He has truly helped me through so much. When we experience trauma, we truly can't imagine anything good happening again. But I allowed myself to take ownership of my story and change. I could not be scared to go after something that everyone deserves. Never shut yourself off from loving and being loved.

Wanting to get justice for something that happened to you is completely normal. I went through a Title IX process at my old school, and they found my abuser not liable because there was not enough "evidence." I was devastated and heartbroken, but the truth is you do not need anyone to validate or acknowledge what happened to you. My purpose for going on was to accomplish my dream of becoming a nurse. I was assaulted my sophomore year of college and failed every single one of my classes because I could not stop thinking about it. I decided to move back home and transfer schools. This one thing truly had changed my life.

I thought my life would look a different way, and I blamed myself for the longest time, but the truth is no one expects to have this happen to them. I wasn't going to let that monster take that away from me as well. I want to become a nurse so I can help those in times of need. Like I said before, healing takes time, and wow, is that statement true. I was assaulted two years ago and I still think about it, but rather than let it consume me I allow myself to feel those uncomfortable feelings and process them. If you are feeling frustrated and think you should be "over it," please know there is no timeline. You have the right to take as much time as you need. Take it from someone like me. I have seen many counselors and taken many anti-anxiety meds, but once we allow ourselves to process those emotions and feelings, they simply become less big. Journaling those feelings you hold in your mind is something that has helped me find peace, and leaning on the people who you love and who love you is something that is essential. My message to anyone who may be reading this is never underestimate your power. My hope is that one day we allow survivors to step out of the shadows and into the light. No one should feel ashamed or scared for something they had no control over. There is strength in owning your story.

Love,

Steven

LET'S CHECK IN

Making the decision to seek justice for your assault can be overwhelming. There's a lot to think about and perhaps more options than you feel you can consider in the moment. There's no rush to do so. Here are some practices that can help you process:

- Get a sheet of paper and a pen, set a timer for two minutes, and write down every thought and question you have. Just write.

When the time is up, you can review your notes or tear up the page and throw it away.

- Write a list of pros and cons about reporting. Using a scale of 1 to 5, assign a weight to each item, with 5 being a higher priority/weight and 1 being the lowest. Take time to think through the "why" of each item, its placement on the list, and the weight you're assigning it. For example,

Pros:
  ○ I would know that I held my perpetrator accountable to the best of my ability.—5 (this is *very* important to me)
  ○ I might have the opportunity to share my story in court.—4 (this is important to me)

Cons:
  ○ I would have to disclose my story to other people, and I am not sure I am ready yet.—4 (this is a big concern for me)
  ○ I know the process is lengthy.—2 (this is not a big concern for me)

- Look up the closest sexual assault advocacy center and save its contact information. It never hurts to have this on hand.

Reporting is the start of a new, potentially long journey that includes its own set of challenges and milestones. Consider what's most important to *you* and put yourself and your needs first. Take all the time you need to process, and be sure to incorporate self-care activities. You made it this far, and you can keep going.

In Part II, we looked at how to build our formal and informal support team and how to disclose and report our trauma in detail. A big weight we carry as sexual assault survivors is knowing who to tell and how to tell them about what happened to us. Take time to review this information as many times as you need in order to feel you can make an informed decision. In Part III, you'll find more information about what happens after making the report to law enforcement and how to navigate the judicial system.

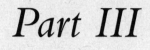

Part III

CHAPTER 8

The Investigation

In a criminal investigation, law enforcement collects evidence showing that a crime was committed, looks for motives, and investigates the person accused of committing the crime. While it may seem like the victim would be very involved in the investigation, it's more common for survivors to be relatively uninvolved in this process. It can be hard to stand by while the investigation takes place, but you won't have much of an idea what's happening. If you think that waiting for updates about the investigation and waiting for it to end might increase your anxiety, do your best to focus on yourself and your own healing during this time.

Typically, your role in the investigation begins by providing the initial statement when you report the crime. You may also need to answer follow-up questions and might be interviewed multiple times. But in some cases, the victim isn't asked for additional information.

After making the report, you might not have much contact with law enforcement while they work the investigation. Any assistance you can provide by continuing to answer their questions and also offering additional relevant information can influence whether the prosecution will move forward with your case.

During the investigation of my case, waiting for more information was unbearable at times. I couldn't stop worrying, and I kept imagining every potential scenario or conversation that could happen. I remember the dread that filled me when I thought about law enforcement reaching out to the person who raped me and how he would react when he found out I had reported the crime. It's normal to experience a wide range of emotions during the investigation—anger, anxiety, sadness; you may even feel satisfaction that your case is being pursued. No matter how you feel, your primary role during the investigation is to take care of yourself. Establish health and safety routines that support your mental, emotional, and physical health. As we discussed in chapter five, you get to decide who you disclose details of your case to, and you choose where to put boundaries in place around what you share.

EXPERT CONTRIBUTION: THE INTERVIEW AND INVESTIGATION
Retired Detective Justin Boardman, of Boardman Training and Consulting

Sadly, victims who choose to participate in the justice system should expect a variety of responses, some good and some not so good. With so many disciplines involved in the process, including law enforcement, victim advocates, forensic nurses, and prosecution, you will be interviewed about your experience several times. Understandably, this raises a host of issues. Sometimes our memories can change, miscommunication can occur between disciplines, and talking about the experience time after time just, plainly spoken, sucks!

To begin with, you should be treated respectfully by the professionals you interact with, and they should believe that something horrible happened to you. They should also provide you with privacy and plenty of time to communicate with them. Investigating intimate crimes is a marathon and not a sprint.

When the person talks with you, they should be using language that is non-blaming and not minimizing your experience. While communicating, they should give you prompts to talk, then give you the space and time to describe the event. This will help you access your thoughts and feelings about what happened to you and provide additional mental safety to express yourself. Sensory memories are often difficult to talk about, but essential because they provide more insight and can sometimes be corroborated for the investigation.

The investigation process has several steps, and a variety of people will be involved. The following summarizes what you can typically expect during the interviewing and investigation process.

Call Taker. A call taker is a member of the law enforcement community whose job is to gather information quickly, respectfully, and in ways that promote feelings of safety. They need to find out about any safety concerns for you and the officers that will be responding. Most have a script they read from and don't have much wiggle room to deviate until they finish the questions. They need to determine if you were injured and if you're physically safe and then evaluate whether a medical response is necessary. Law enforcement should always be dispatched to assess the next steps in the investigation.

During the conversation with you, the call taker should affirm that you are not responsible for what has happened to you, express empathy, and give you an estimated time for contact by the police. They should also try not to ask about the details of your assault, except for response needs, medical, and safety concerns. That said, don't worry about sharing too much. It is natural and more than okay.

Initial Police Response. Depending on the circumstances of your assault, the response of the police could be in person or over the phone. The officer who talks to you should focus first on your safety and well-being. That said, just like fingerprints, every case the officer investigates is different, so they must make decisions based on various facts, which can get complicated. They may also contact others with more experience, like a detective or supervisor. This is a good thing. You may feel nervous, but the officer is ensuring they're handling things the best way as they have been trained.

After discovering your safety issues, they should start finding out about you and building rapport. As a person reporting a crime or interacting with police, you should assume your interaction is recorded by audio or video. This is good because it helps everyone be safe and will be used as evidence for the case. As the officer communicates, they should do so in non-judgmental language, using open-ended questions and letting you speak about your experience. If you have memories that may not seem important to the investigation, these should still be shared or written. The memories that may not seem relevant are often the first to fade, but recalling them can be helpful. Be sure to focus on your feelings and sensations so they are documented. Building cases for the justice system requires the collection of many details.

The officer should also coordinate and provide resources for your geographic location. This may be an advocate working in the department or community advocates and organizations. Advocates are there to help you navigate, but it should be understood that some advocates can share the information with the investigators. If the advocate works for the justice system, they do not have confidentiality requirements and can share what you have told them with investigators. A community advocate *does* retain confidentiality, and they don't share information with investigators unless they obtain permission from you.

Investigative Interview. Depending on numerous factors, an investigative interview may take place a few days to weeks after the event. This is due to different-sized police departments and their structures. If you're worried and would like to call in to find out more, I encourage you to do so. If you have contact with the victim's advocate, they should be helping you stay up to date and find helpful information. For a medium-sized department, more than likely, there will be an investigator assigned to your case. The best practice is to wait a few days after an event for a formal interview. This is due to the trauma in our brains; we need a few sleep cycles to consolidate memories.

The interview should take place in a private and comfortable room. It should be recorded via CCTV and audio. The recording process helps the investigator focus on what you're saying about your experience, and they don't have to take as many notes. This will also be provided in discovery if criminal charges are filed. This is a good thing; it will show the harm their client has caused. Like the other disciplines, the investigative interviewer should help to give you a personal sense of safety. This will go hand-in-hand with time to explain what happened to you. You should schedule a lot of time for a formal interview, a few hours at least. It may not take that long, but your brain may not release some memories if it's worried you have another appointment to get to.

A support person can help you feel more comfortable sharing your experience. This may be harder than you think. You may feel guilty if someone wants to help and you don't feel comfortable enough around them to share, or maybe the particular person you wish to have has a busy schedule. Best practices would point to having the victim's advocate present with you during the interview. Victim advocates are trained to be in these interviews and know the system, and are there only in your interest. This is important and can help form a bond and rapport that will serve as support throughout the investigation and possibly court. Bringing in friends, parents, or even significant others is not always wise. You may feel embarrassed about situations or details and be reluctant to share them in front of people you know. And sometimes the details of the event can affect relationships in ways that can't be predicted, so having a victim advocate with you is usually the best option.

The investigator should spend time with you and get to know you before asking questions about the event. Establishing rapport is extremely important to build trust, help you feel safe, and increase the details your brain may give up during the interview. When the investigator moves toward the central part of the interview, they should let you speak uninterrupted for as long as you want. They may jot down a few notes to get back to and ask questions about. Talking to you and asking questions in a tone that doesn't increase your anxiety or shame is extremely important. If this is not being done, the victim advocate should remind the investigator. It is essential to understand that they sometimes have to ask hard questions. Some of these hard questions are not always trauma-informed, but sadly, they are necessary. Questions may include how much you had to drink or why you decided to do something. Investigators need to get this information, not to embarrass you, but to ensure they're prepared for the suspect's interview and the details that the defense presents. It is part of the process. So, if a detail comes to mind during the interview, do your best to share it.

In the interview, investigators are looking for the "elements" of the offense they are investigating. Because most sexual assault crimes are committed by victims' acquaintances, the defense will say the suspect "thought it was consensual." It's okay if you didn't say "no" or fight back. Please give as much detail as you can, including how it felt to be assaulted. In hindsight, you may be embarrassed or mad about the way you responded to the trauma, but your response is not your fault; it's what your brain decided *before* the event happened. If you felt you were going to die at the time, then say it. Even if you look back now and think, "I wouldn't have died." The investigator needs to figure out why you didn't resist, yell out, or run away. Sometimes they don't have the experience to explain this with much tact. So, if it comes to your mind while talking, please tell them.

The investigator should ask follow-up questions about how you felt during a portion of the event or what you remember smelling during or after. Recalling scents and odors helps the brain to access memories that are recorded in your brain along with other feelings and sensations.

The police investigate crimes, but don't do much with the person who made the report after the interview. Wrapping up the investigative interview, the investigator should ask how you would like to be contacted in the future. Sometimes people don't like phone calls or text messages. So be sure to share your preferences. If you don't already have an advocate, they should also introduce you to one. This is extremely important, because the advocate will do more to support you through the process than the police. Sometimes it's also a good idea to give the investigator another person's contact information, like a parent, sibling, or close friend, in case yours is lost. After the interview, if you remember more details, even if it's weeks later, be sure to pass these along to the investigator. They may be the key to charges.

Investigators are usually extremely busy and rarely pass along information about the timeline or how the investigation is proceeding. If you need information or want to know the status of your case, it's fine to contact them. Email is a good option because it documents the request. If the investigator doesn't reply, you can forward the initial email to your victim advocate or even their supervisor. Most of the time, that is not needed. Being trauma-informed, they would reach out to you more often, but most of the time, investigators won't unless they've made an arrest or received a declination from the prosecutor's office.

TAKING CARE OF YOURSELF DURING AN INVESTIGATION

Every investigation is unique, but there are some practices that can be helpful to all survivors during this time.

There's no way of knowing how long the investigation is going to take, and it's important not to put your healing process on hold while it takes place. In addition to working through the trauma of your assault with a mental health professional, it's vital to learn strong coping and emotional regulation skills as you prepare for the potential of going to court and the ups and downs that go with it. To navigate the emotions that can be triggered by not having control and feeling left in the dark, my number one suggestion is to go to therapy as much as possible. If you were seeing a therapist prior to your assault, it may be helpful for you to start seeing them more often, perhaps twice a week if that is affordable and feasible for you. As we talked about in chapter six, adding a therapist to your support team can be a great benefit. Having someone hold space for all your emotions, anxieties, and questions will help you to feel safe enough to process the array of thoughts and feelings that you're experiencing.

If the cost of therapy is stopping you from receiving services, talk to your victim advocate or someone from your local law enforcement about how to access crime victim compensation, which is financial reimbursement for expenses that occur because of the crime. As the compensation is related to the crime committed, a report to law enforcement is necessary to access this funding.

Your victim advocate and local law enforcement will be able to tell you what agency you need to contact to apply for this compensation, but here is the process in general:

- You must report your crime to law enforcement.
- You must be working with law enforcement regarding your case.
- Submit the application in a timely manner (what is considered timely will vary in each compensation program).

States vary in what costs they cover, but federal law requires all states to have compensation programs that cover crime-related costs for lost wages, medical treatment, and mental health counseling. No amount of reimbursement can cover the way our lives have been altered by the trauma of sexual assault; however, it's still worth accessing the resources available to help you. Your future, your health, and your healing are worth it.

If you don't feel comfortable reaching out to your local law enforcement for crime victim compensation, you may want to learn more about the mental health clinics in your area that offer sliding fee scales, which means the fees are based on your income and ability to pay for therapy services.

Managing Anxiety During the Investigation

Everyone processes trauma differently, but many of us feel more secure and safe when we have all the facts and can control a situation. Because sexual assault strips away our sense of control, the lack of control we have over the investigation can create a lot of anxiety for us, as well as for our friends and family members who want to support and protect us.

Lean on the support team you've created. It can be hard to ask for help, and if you feel asking for help is too challenging, consider reaching out to someone and asking to simply go on a walk or see a movie together. Consider what practices have helped you with anxiety in the past. For example, some people find that keeping a full and structured weekly plan is helpful. See what areas of your life you can gain more control over in a healthy way. Will meal planning or time-blocking your day relieve some anxiety? Will getting your clothes ready for the next day make it easier to start the day?

You can also schedule check-in times with your victim advocate or with the law enforcement team assigned to your case. You can let them know that you'd like updates when something new occurs. Or you can ask them to communicate with you on a biweekly basis, even if the email or message from them says there are no updates at this time. If the established timeframe passes without hearing from them, it's okay to respectfully request an update.

Safety Planning

During the investigation, the perpetrator is not permitted to contact you, and none of the people they know should contact you about the investigation. You have a right during the investigation and trial to have reasonable protection provided.[27] Ask law enforcement how they will provide this protection to you. If someone reaches out to you in a threatening manner or in a way that's inappropriate for the case, contact your local law enforcement immediately. (For more information regarding safety planning, see chapter two).

PROSECUTING THE CRIME

Law enforcement investigates the case, and if the team decides it meets the standard of probable cause, they send the case file to the prosecuting attorney along with evidence they gathered, including statements from witnesses and physical evidence. The prosecuting attorney decides whether to move forward with filing the case against the accused person. More is covered by Melissa Hoppmeyer and Kathryn Marsh later in this chapter regarding the prosecution taking a case to court.

In the criminal court process, the prosecuting attorney might include you in making the decision about whether the case will proceed to trial. If they don't, ideally, they'll explain how they came to their decision and give you a chance to ask questions and process the decision. Prosecuting attorneys rarely take a case to trial without the victim's agreement, but it can happen. No matter what decision is reached, you'll probably need time to process it and consider what's next. We'll talk briefly here about the two possible outcomes; in the next chapter, we'll explore specifics about the criminal trial process.

When the case goes to trial. Even if you were hoping charges would be filed, when you find out your case will be proceeding to trial, you may feel some fear, anxiety, doubt, or even moments of regret. If you have moments when you wonder if you've made the right choice, remember how hard you fought to reach this point and that by continuing to move forward and fight for yourself, you're also fighting for all survivors who didn't have the opportunity to see their cases move forward. In an ideal world, every survivor would have their day in court.

When the case doesn't go to trial. Learning that your case won't be going to trial can be devastating. Grief, anger, and confusion are just a few of the emotions you might initially feel. You might feel like all your efforts were wasted, you weren't believed, or your perpetrator won. Take time to honor these feelings, as these emotions exist from the part of you that knows you deserve more and feels unheard.

Whether or not the state chooses to file criminal charges, you have the option to hire an attorney and take your case to civil court. You also have the option to step away from the stress that pursuing legal action can cause and focus on your healing. Ultimately, what matters most is finding a way to continue moving forward and building a full life for yourself. That might not sound possible right now. But with work, intention, and healing, your life will take shape in so many new ways. If this is what you decide to do, skip to Part IV, where you can create a healing plan with the practices, techniques, and other modalities that best fit you.

EXPERT CONTRIBUTION: TAKING THE CASE TO TRIAL
Kathryn Marsh, Esq., and Melissa Hoppmeyer, Esq.

Only 310 sexual assaults out of every 1,000 are reported.[28] On average, only 50 out of the 310 reports, or 16 percent of reported sexual assaults, lead to an arrest.[29]

So, where's the disconnect? Why do so few of the reported sexual assaults lead to an arrest or prosecution? In some cases, the suspect is unknown and therefore no one can be charged. In other cases, the victim and the physical evidence may not be able to explain what specific sexual acts were committed. This may happen when the victim of a sexual assault is under the influence of an intoxicating substance. Although the victim knows something happened, they may not be able to provide actual details of penetration or other sexual acts. Generally, a criminal charge of sexual assault requires the prosecution to prove a specific act occurred such as: penetration of the vulva by a penis, finger, or tongue. Without the evidence to prove a specific act, the prosecution can't file charges.

But what about when the suspect is known or a specific sexual act is described? Why aren't all of these cases prosecuted? This section will explore the ethical and legal standards prosecutors must consider in deciding to charge and in ultimately trying a case. While there are many reasons a prosecutor may not be able to charge or ultimately try a sexual assault case, the inability to charge does not mean that the victim is not believed. We hope this will help explain why prosecutors may not charge a sexual assault.

Role of the Prosecutor

Prosecutors are charged with the highest ethical standards and for good reason. Prosecutors determine what charges to bring, how to try the criminal case, and what sentence to request from the court. Prosecutors must be fair and honest in the execution of these duties. In 1935, the US Supreme Court defined the role of a prosecutor as not to win a case but to see that justice shall be done.[30] Prosecutors must weigh what is in the best interests of the community, the victim, the accused, and the criminal justice system when making their charging decisions. Although it may seem counterintuitive for the prosecutor to consider the best interests of the accused, there are factors including mental health, addiction, and the age of the accused that are considered when the prosecutor determines what the just result of any given case should be.

When to Charge

The American Bar Association Criminal Justice Standards for Prosecution Function states: "A prosecutor should seek or file criminal charges only if the prosecutor reasonably believes that the charges are supported by probable cause, *that admissible evidence will be sufficient to support conviction beyond a reasonable doubt*, and that the decision to charge is in the interests of justice."[31]

We hear the words "probable cause" and "beyond a reasonable doubt" all the time, but what do they really mean, and how do they apply in the criminal justice system? Probable cause simply means that a crime probably happened and that the person charged probably committed the crime. Probable cause is required for a search warrant or a simple arrest, but mere probable cause will not support a criminal conviction.

Beyond a reasonable doubt is the highest standard of proof in the American court systems. In its most simple terms, this means that "the prosecution must convince the jury [or judge] that there is no other reasonable explanation that can come from the evidence presented at trial,"[32] other than that the accused committed the crime for which they are on trial.

A person can be arrested for a sexual assault when there is probable cause, but a prosecutor should not indict or try the case unless they have admissible evidence to support a conviction beyond a reasonable doubt. This does not mean that a prosecutor should not charge and try the tough or borderline cases. They absolutely should. But they just need to be sure they have the necessary admissible evidence to support a conviction.

What is Evidence?

Evidence can be direct or circumstantial, and a judge or jury can give equal weight to both types. Direct evidence may be the testimony of the victim who positively identifies the accused as the person who sexually assaulted them. Direct evidence may also be DNA results, a confession, a video of the assault, or any other piece of evidence that directly ties the accused to the crime. Circumstantial evidence is indirect evidence that creates the logical inference of a certain fact. Consider a typical winter night in the northern part of the US. Someone is getting ready to go to bed and is watching the news where the weatherman says it is going to snow overnight. They check the temperature and see that it's 20 degrees outside. When they wake up in the morning, they see a foot of snow on the ground. Since they had been sleeping, they did not see it snow, but the circumstantial evidence, including the weather report, the temperature, and the snow on the ground, demonstrates that it did, in fact, snow.

In most cases, there is a lot of evidence such as: statements of a victim; witnesses; medical records; DNA results; text messages; surveillance cameras; and more. Prior to a criminal trial, defense attorneys will generally file motions with the court to try to suppress evidence. This can include motions to suppress confessions, evidence seized by law enforcement, and scientific testing that may not meet scientific or national standards. If a court suppresses the evidence, meaning the prosecution wouldn't be able to use the evidence at trial, or a witness is no longer available, the prosecutor needs to evaluate the case as if the evidence or witness statement never existed in the first place. If the prosecutor cannot support a conviction beyond a reasonable doubt without the suppressed or missing evidence, the prosecutor should not take the case to trial. This can be devastating for the victim, as it is not the victim's fault the evidence was suppressed.

There is also evidence that may not be considered by a prosecutor when evaluating charges for a case, no matter how much the prosecutor or victim may want to present it. This may include propensity evidence, which is evidence that tends to show that because the accused committed a similar bad act in the past, it is likely they committed the act they are on trial for as well. It makes sense, if the accused sexually assaulted three other people prior to the sexual assault that they are currently on trial for, one would think the jury should be able to hear and consider this evidence. However, generally this evidence is not admissible at trial as it is deemed too prejudicial to the accused, and therefore the accused would not be able to have a fair trial if the prosecutor were able to discuss propensity evidence. While there are limited exceptions in some jurisdictions that permit some forms of propensity evidence to be admitted at trial, the prosecution must first file a motion and have an evidentiary hearing before the judge, who will determine if the prosecution can prove the propensity evidence by a clear and convincing standard and that the propensity evidence is not unduly prejudicial. Because this is a high bar for prosecutors to meet, they should not rely on propensity evidence when determining whether or not to charge a case.

Interests of Justice

The final factor a prosecutor must consider in charging or proceeding to trial is what is in the best interests of justice. One interests of justice factor that a prosecutor may consider when deciding whether to charge a sexual assault case is the age of the accused and the victim. Consider an eighteen-year-old who's in a romantic relationship with a fifteen-year-old. In some jurisdictions, sex between the two would be a chargeable offense, while in other jurisdictions it would not be chargeable. If the evidence shows that the eighteen- and fifteen-year-old were in a relationship, with permission of their parents, the interests of justice would weigh against charging the eighteen-year-old.

However, in sexual assault cases the interests of justice should always include considering what is best for the victim. Sometimes a victim of sexual assault initially wants to go forward but later decides for their mental health or well-being that they don't want to proceed to trial or have to testify. In other cases, even knowing the case would be extremely difficult to prove to a jury of twelve people, the victim is adamant about having their voice heard in court, and the prosecution should give heavy weight to this interest. In a case of sexual assault, when all other choices have been taken from a victim, a prosecutor should ensure that when the evidence is there, the victim has the choice of proceeding to trial.

Although there are many factors and ethical considerations a prosecutor must consider when deciding whether to charge a crime or proceed to trial, a victim of crime should always have the opportunity to ask questions and have the final decision explained to them.

LET'S CHECK IN

The journey to seek justice can be draining, no matter what the outcome is. Think about what will fill your cup, give you energy, and increase your resilience for the road ahead.

Consider the following:

- What foods will help fuel your body? Fruits, vegetables, and lots of vitamin C can help energize you and ward off illness.
- Can you spend some time in the sun? Even if it's just standing by a window for fifteen minutes.
- What people, animals, or activities make you feel safe and comforted? Surround yourself with photos of them, have conversations with them, and spend time leaning on them.
- What songs can you turn on to find comfort? Close your eyes and sit with the lyrics and music.

Take the time you need, the time you *deserve*, to take care of yourself. And when you're ready, begin with the next chapter that will be most helpful for you.

CHAPTER 9

The Criminal Trial and Testifying

In a criminal trial the prosecuting and defense attorneys present evidence to a judge or judge and jury so they can decide if the person accused of the crime is guilty. The trial also presents an opportunity for the victim to share their story and hold their perpetrator accountable. A criminal trial is a complex process and can be overwhelming, and it'll be hard to explore all the details here. Mostly, it's important for you to know what your rights are during the trial and generally what to expect during the proceedings.

If the prosecution takes the case to court (see chapter eight), there are two types of criminal trial processes, **bench trials** and **jury trials**. The defendant (the one being charged with the crime) is the one who decides which type of trial they want. As the victim of the crime, you do not get to decide if it is a bench trial or jury trial. However, you can make the choice to look into civil court. (See page 195 to learn more about civil court.)

In a bench trial all evidence is presented to a judge, who weighs the evidence, makes the decisions about how to apply the law to the case, and decides if the defendant is guilty.

In a jury trial the evidence is presented to a group of citizens selected by the prosecuting and defense attorneys, and those citizens become the jury and determine the verdict.

While there are often unexpected twists and turns in a trial, the basics covered in this chapter will help you to be more prepared for what's ahead.

LEADING UP TO A CRIMINAL TRIAL

After the investigation has concluded and the accused has been charged with a crime, there will be several hearings before the trial takes place. Your victim advocate will help you decide if you should attend these hearings, but victims typically do not have to attend. Leading up to the trial, the prosecution and defense teams will be examining their evidence and preparing their case. The prosecution may reach out to you with questions while they prepare, but you might not hear from them until right before the trial. When a trial date is set, you'll receive a subpoena, or notice, for when you're required to appear in court.

Waiting for the trial date to be set and for the trial to begin might increase your anxiety, especially since the trial date can be pushed back a few times, and it sometimes happens at the last minute. You can ask the prosecution team that's representing your case or your victim advocate if they have insight or thoughts about whether the trial date might be postponed.

EXPERT CONTRIBUTION: COURTROOM DEFENSES AND RAPE MYTHS
Melissa Hoppmeyer, Esq., and Kathryn Marsh, Esq.

If a criminal case makes it to the courtroom for trial, the difficulties for the victim survivor unfortunately are not over. Rape myths are prevalent throughout our society, and the courtroom is no exception. This section will explore both legal and non-legal defenses that play out in courtrooms across the country. We hope this will help arm you with information as you talk to your prosecutor about trial and help you as you navigate the difficult criminal justice system.

Before we get started on rape myths in the courtroom, it's important to note that the criminal justice system is an adversarial process and one designed specifically and constitutionally to protect the rights of the accused. This constitutional protection is sacred but creates a system designed to protect defendants, not victim survivors. This is difficult to understand, but these constitutional protections protect all criminal defendants and are the bedrock of our democracy. Defense attorneys' use of both legal and non-legal defenses are intertwined with these rights, but preparation with your prosecutor can help when it comes to trial.

Consent

A legal defense to sexual assault and rape is consent. The defense of consent simply boils down to both parties agreed to engage in the sexual contact or act. But if you are reading this book, you know it is just not that simple. There are many definitions of consent; in fact, several states, including Wisconsin, Florida, and California, have enacted legal definitions of consent. This is a law that tells a jury or judge what consent means. However, more than half of the fifty states still do not define consent in their laws, leaving consent open to interpretation by attorneys and jurors. If you want information about your state's consent laws, look at RAINN's defining consent database, which is a great resource.

If, at its most basic, consent is an agreement freely entered into by two parties, then when doesn't consent exist? When you are defining or determining consent as a prosecutor, you must analyze first whether the victim survivor had the ability to consent. Intoxication, level of consciousness, age, mental disabilities, and even potentially the defendant's position of authority all impact a prosecutor's assessment of consent. It is important to note that your individual state law will impact this assessment. Make sure to discuss this with your prosecutor as you are preparing for trial.

The Liar

While consent is a legal defense to sexual assault or rape, the trope regarding the victim survivor's veracity or ability to tell the truth is a commonly used non-legal defense to sexual assault. Defense attorneys use the rape myth that victims lie about sexual assault because they have regret. This misconception is pervasive in our society and plays well in front of juries. Defense attorneys will use perceived "inconsistencies" from the victim survivor's multiple statements to showcase to the jury that the victim is dishonest and should not be believed. This is why trauma-informed investigations are crucial to the success of sexual assault cases. Limiting the number of times the victim survivor has to tell their story and using open-ended questions to clarify perceived inconsistencies prior to trial can go a long way.

It's also important to note that false reports of sexual assault or rape are exceedingly rare. In fact, study after study, according to the National Sexual Violence Resource Center, have demonstrated that the average rate of false report for sexual assault or rape is approximately 5 to 8 percent. Said conversely, that means approximately 92 to 95 percent of all sexual assault reports are true. For a more detailed explanation about the rates of false reports, check out a helpful legal

article, "False Reports: Moving Beyond the Issue to Successfully Investigate and Prosecute Non-Stranger Sexual Assault" by Dr. Lonsway,
Sgt. Archambault, and Dr. Lisak.[33] The truth is that false reports of
sexual assault and rape occur at no higher rate than false reports of any
other violent crime. It is incumbent on the prosecutors in your jurisdiction to combat this rape myth both in individual trials and as a community advocate by presenting the truths about rape myths.

Victim Blaming

Another non-legal defense is the defense of victim blaming: shifting
the burden of wrongdoing from the defendant to the victim. Ideas
that the victim's behavior, actions, inactions, or dress caused the sexual
assault. Defense attorneys consistently argue that the victim should not
have gone to the defendant's house or room if they did not intend to
have sexual contact or engage in sexual acts. Or they will argue that the
victim's clothing played a direct role in their sexual assault and that
the victim needs to accept some level of responsibility for what occurred.
This rape myth rears its ugly head in many sexual assault or rape trials and is incredibly damaging to the victim survivor and to society at
large because it creates this false narrative that victims are to blame for
a defendant's actions.

We want to be clear, when we discuss shifting the burden of blame,
we are not talking about the burden of proof. The government has the
burden of proving the defendant guilty beyond a reasonable doubt,
and the defendant has no obligation to prove his or her innocence of
the charges. The government should be steadfast in its ownership of the
burden of proof; however, it should be equally steadfast in dispelling
victim-blaming rape myths. The prosecutor should educate the jury on

the elements of the crime of sexual assault or rape and any defenses. It is important to build and present the case to the jury with a focus on the defendant and their actions, not on the actions of the victim. The prosecutor can do this in direct examination of the victim survivor, through alternative witnesses, including expert witnesses, and throughout closing arguments.

"They Don't Look Like a Rapist"

We are a society that focuses on image. We often jump to conclusions about a person's values and personality based upon their appearance. This remains true inside of a courtroom. Jurors and judges all come with their own personal biases and will judge an individual based upon their appearance. This extends to defendants and the universal rape myth that a rapist looks a certain way. As a society, we want to believe that we can identify predators by their appearance. We don't want to believe that rapists walk among us undetected and can be members of our families. Defense attorneys know this myth and will play up the clean-cut looks of a defendant at trial. It is not uncommon to see a defendant with a fresh haircut, wearing a suit, and carrying a Bible at trial, trying to look like an upstanding member of society. The ugly truth is that you cannot judge a book by its cover, and rapists do walk among us. The idea that someone looks or doesn't look like they are capable of violence needs to be combatted by the prosecutor. Again, through education of the jury or judge, the prosecutor is responsible for presenting facts that dispel this rape myth. It is also important that the victim survivor and the prosecutor have the tough conversation about appearances as well, because just as the jury and judge will make judgments about the defendant, they will also make judgments about the victim.

Mistake of Fact

Another legal defense sometimes available to defendants is the defense of mistake of fact. Mistake of fact is the legal concept that the defendant reasonably believed that the victim consented or was able to consent. Much like our discussion on consent, this defense uses rape myths to develop a legally sufficient defense. Defense attorneys will use the victim survivor's actions, past and present, as well as their dress, to make legal claims that if consent was not given by the victim survivor, then the defendant reasonably believed that the victim consented and is not guilty of the sexual assault or rape. This mistake of fact defense is not allowed in many jurisdictions but is important to discuss, because unlike other defenses discussed, the jury is instructed on this defense. It is important to use facts to dispel the ability for a juror to believe the defendant *reasonably* believed the victim was capable of consent. This is especially true when the case involves drugs or alcohol, and the victim survivor was incapable of consent because of intoxication.

"Only Women Can Be Raped"

Another problematic rape myth that permeates the courtroom is that only women can be victim survivors of rape or sexual assault. We know this is patently false and comes from patriarchal ideas and laws that classified victims of sexual assault and rape as women. Our laws are only starting to catch up with the truth that victim survivors can be all genders, sexual orientations, and backgrounds. Many states even up until recently defined rape as vaginal penetration by a penis or an object. This obviously left out a large portion of the population that experienced sexual violence. As laws catch up to reality, we still need to ensure we are cognizant that, although laws are changing, our juries and judges may continue to hold these beliefs. Experts can assist in helping to explain this rape myth to juries and judges, and it is imperative for prosecutors to work with victim survivors to prepare them for questioning on the stand.

"Rape Is Rare"

One of the most prevalent rape myths is the idea that rape is rare in our society and perpetrated by deviant defendants who jump out of bushes. This myth is perpetuated by the media and pop culture. This idea that rape happens only in dark alleys and involves the use of weapons is incredibly inaccurate and misleading. The sad truth is that rape is pervasive in our society. In fact, one in six women and one in thirty-three men will experience sexual assault or rape in their lifetime. And 80.5 percent of perpetrators are known to victims.[34] This is one of the most difficult rape myths to tackle because it's a larger societal issue that cannot be combatted with facts related to the individual case. The truth of the matter is that we have to work to raise this issue as a country. The #MeToo movement has helped, but we need to continue to voice the truth. Although battling rape myths may appear daunting, special victim prosecutors are trained to combat these defenses in the courtroom.

JURY TRIAL: WHAT TO EXPECT

The criminal trial process isn't the same everywhere, so be sure to ask a victim advocate or sexual assault advocate in the jurisdiction where the crime occurred to explain the specifics of their process. The following is general information about the stages of a jury trial and the people involved.

Who Will Be in the Courtroom

To increase your comfort in the courtroom, ask your advocate if you can visit before the trial and also ask who you can bring with you to the trial for support. Friends and family can usually attend the trial, but if they're witnesses they won't be able to attend the entire trial because they're not permitted in the courtroom prior to giving their testimony. In many jurisdictions, sexual assault trials are open to the public, including media, unless there are restrictions that have been put in place by the judge to limit the public from being in attendance.

On the first day of trial, ask your advocate to point out and identify the professionals in the courtroom and tell you what their roles are in the trial. In addition to you and the defendant, you can expect to see:

Judge. The judge interprets the law and how it applies to the case. Judges can be elected by voters, chosen by a committee, or appointed by the governor. Ideally, the judge has experience in criminal law and sexual violence criminal law, but not all states require judges to have that experience.

Defense attorney. The defense attorney is there to advocate and advise their client, present evidence that strengthens their case, and cross-examine witnesses. Their job is to protect their client's rights and ensure they receive a fair trial.

The prosecuting attorney. The prosecuting attorney represents the government during the trial. They might be referred to as a prosecutor or district/assistant district attorney. Although they don't represent the victim of the crime, they typically will keep you informed about the proceedings of the case. Their primary role is to pursue the criminal charges against those who have committed crimes. They will have worked with law enforcement to investigate the crime and determine if there's sufficient evidence to charge the suspect. They then present this information to the judge or jury to seek a conviction. They can also negotiate plea bargains.

The jury. In a jury trial, the members of the jury listen to the evidence presented by both the prosecutor and the defense and determine if the accused person is guilty of the crimes they've been charged with. They listen to the witness testimonies, review any physical evidence, and consider arguments presented by both attorneys. They must make their decision based on the evidence presented in court, and not on any outside factors or personal biases they have.

The bailiff. The bailiff is a law enforcement officer who maintains order and security in the courtroom. They will also assist the judge and escort defendants to and from the courtroom if necessary.

The court reporter. The court reporter documents every word that is said during the trial and creates a transcript of the trial.

The clerk of the court. The court clerk will be involved in administering oaths, numbering exhibits that are entered, and maintaining court documents.

The victim witness/advocate. The victim witness/advocate is a professional who supports the victim throughout the trial process. Please see chapter two for more information about the roles of this profession.

THE STAGES OF THE JURY TRIAL

If yours will be a jury trial, you can increase your comfort level by learning how a jury trial works and how it will proceed. First, jury selection. In this process, potential jurors are selected from a pool of eligible citizens. The process may vary in each jurisdiction, but some common steps are:

1. Jurors are selected from a pool of eligible individuals, which is typically created from a source or database such as voter registration lists.

2. Each individual receives a summons, informing them that they're obligated to appear for jury duty on a specific date.

3. The potential jurors are shown the courthouse and informed about the trial process and their roles and responsibilities as a jury member.

4. They may fill out a questionnaire to provide basic information, such as their background, education, and occupation.

5. The potential jurors then go through the *voir dire* process, in which they're questioned by the prosecution and defense teams to determine if they're suitable to be a jury member on the case. The goal of this process is to identify any biases or conflicts of interest. Each attorney has their own agenda for how they decide if they want someone sitting on the jury.

6. Attorneys can challenge or request the removal of certain potential jurors by presenting their reasoning to the judge.

7. After the challenges are completed, the remaining potential individuals are selected to be on the jury.

8. The jurors are sworn in and swear to be impartial when considering the evidence and choosing a verdict based on the law.

9. A foreperson will be selected. Typically, jurors are allowed to volunteer for the role. Ultimately, the selection is up to the judge presiding over the trial.

Reasons someone might be excused from being on the jury include:

- They know one of the witnesses.
- They have been sexually assaulted.
- They are in a career that might cause them to have a bias.
- They have a schedule conflict that they absolutely cannot work around. Examples include surgery, military duty, or being a full-time student.

Since you are also a witness to the crime, you are not always allowed to attend the jury selection process. There may be exceptions to this; for example, you may be requested to be present during the voir dire process so that the jury can be asked if they know or recognize you.

If you're given the option to attend the voir dire process, consider these questions:

- Will having time in the courtroom help you gain familiarity with the room and ease some anxiety?
- Will it be beneficial or cause you more anxiety to see your perpetrator before you testify?
- Would your time be better spent practicing self-care?

IF YOU'RE EVER A JUROR

Jury selection is an important process to help determine if you're suitable to sit on the jury. It's important to be honest about whether you will be able to remain impartial during the trial. Instead of thinking of how jury duty is going to be an inconvenience, consider that you're there to help determine justice. Imagine it's your family member who has been the victim of a crime and how much courage it would take to be willing to go to court.

Being a member of a jury is one of a citizen's most important responsibilities, and many people find it very empowering. The judge, the lawyers, and the witnesses won't determine the outcome of the trial—you will.

Trial Proceedings

After the trial has begun and the jury has been selected, the first order of business will be **opening statements**. These prepare the jury for what they will hear and see during the trial. During the opening statements, the prosecution presents an overview of the charges the defendant is accused of, and the defense outlines their strategy to challenge the case that the prosecution is presenting. Each jurisdiction varies on whether they allow witnesses to sit in during the opening statements. Some courts do not permit witnesses to listen to the opening statements because it could affect the witness's testimony.

After the opening statements, the prosecution offers the **presentation of evidence** that supports their case. This includes witness testimony (including your testimony), physical evidence, and expert opinions. The defense cross-examines the prosecution's witnesses and then presents its own evidence (which the prosecution will then have an opportunity to cross-examine). The defendant also may choose to testify at this time, but they can also choose to remain silent.

After the evidence is presented, the attorneys give their **closing arguments**. These arguments summarize the evidence presented and argue how the case has, or has not, been proven beyond reasonable doubt.

Trials can last days, or they can last weeks. No two trials are the same, and it is difficult to predict how long the trial will take.

Jury Instructions and Deliberation

Jury instructions are a set of standards that jurors use when considering evidence, testimony, and a verdict. The jury instructions will include:

- The explanation of the applicable legal principles of the charges involved in the case and the legal standards that the jury must use to assess the evidence that was presented.
- What the burden of proof is for the case (in sexual assault cases this will be beyond reasonable doubt).
- The principle that the jury must presume innocence unless the prosecution was able to prove otherwise.
- Instructions on the importance of collective decision-making, respectful discussion, and for all jurors to consider the viewpoints of others during the deliberations.

After the evidence and closing arguments are presented and the jury is given their instructions, they **deliberate**, discussing the case and whether they think there is enough evidence for the defendant to be guilty beyond a reasonable doubt. This deliberation can take hours or weeks, depending on the case and the jurors' differing opinions.

After deliberation, the jury returns to the courtroom, and the foreperson of the jury—who the jury chooses from among themselves—reads the verdict. (The verdict and sentencing process are covered in chapter ten.)

SEEING YOUR PERPETRATOR IN COURT

The possibility of seeing the person who assaulted you can be a cause for great anxiety. Your first step should be to work with your therapist on this, who can help you identify and sort out some of those potential emotions ahead of time. It can also be empowering to focus on the opportunity you have to seek justice by telling your story and holding the perpetrator accountable for what they did. No matter what verdict the judge or jury delivers, sitting in front of the person who harmed you and telling a room full of people what happened while under oath can be a significant step in your healing journey.

Some things to prepare for:

- In the courtroom, once you're on the stand, the prosecutor will ask you to identify the person who committed the crime against you. This will probably be the only time you will be asked to acknowledge that he/she/they are in the room unless the judge or the defense attorney requests that you identify them again later.
- If it's easier, don't look at or acknowledge your perpetrator during your testimony after you have identified them.
- The perpetrator might have people supporting them in the courtroom.
- The perpetrator won't be required to testify but might choose to. You are not required to listen to the defendant's testimony, but any victim testifying in the trial has the right to attend public court proceedings. The only exception is if a judge believes listening to other witnesses' testimony will affect your testimony. But most likely you will have already testified because the prosecution presents its case before

the defense, which is when the defendant can testify. Talk to your victim advocate to decide whether staying or leaving will be better for you.

TESTIFYING

It's normal to feel nervous before testifying, so keeping up your self-care practices and using coping and grounding techniques can be very helpful. Beyond taking care of yourself and relying on your support team, there are also some other details you'll want to take care of ahead of time, like choosing outfits for court that are clean, neat, and professional. Your attorney will probably suggest that you wear business clothing or business casual. It's a good idea to try on the outfits you're considering ahead of time to make sure you like how they look and that they feel comfortable. If you don't have something appropriate to wear, reach out to your victim advocate and see if your community has resources to provide you with appropriate clothing for free or minimal cost.

Discuss the rights you'll have during the trial with the prosecuting attorney and your victim advocate. The prosecutor may also review your testimony with you and have some last-minute questions. The prosecutor will not review your testimony in any amount of detail that might suggest they're coaching you before the trial.

Tips for Testifying

In the days before the trial, surround yourself with people who support you, and lean on that support. Do what you can to relax, release stress, sleep, and eat nutritious meals. It can be hard to think about anything besides the upcoming trial, but do your best to keep up all the healthy practices that help you feel good.

- Remember it's the prosecutor's role to help you move through your testimony and share your truth. You are not expected to know everything that's important to say. The prosecutor will ask you questions that give you the opportunity to tell the court what happened to you, and make sure you cover the key points that the jury needs to hear.
- If English is not your first language, you have the right to an interpreter.
- If you need to pause, you can take a few deep breaths and take a sip of water.
- If you feel overwhelmed and need a break, you can request one.
- You can ask for a question to be repeated.
- You can say that you don't understand the question.
- Use your own words and avoid sounding technical or using legal words you are not familiar with.
- You will be asked to be detailed. For example, if you say, "He/she assaulted me," you will be asked to clarify. For example, "He put his penis in my vagina/anus/mouth."
- Be honest. If you do not remember something specific, it's okay to say that. For example, "I don't remember the exact date but I remember walking through slush on my way home and I was at school so it would have been during the spring of last year."
- Remember your testimony is important, and you are being brave by sharing it.

More advice regarding testifying from both prosecution and civil attorneys is presented at the end of this chapter.

The Cross-Examination

Along with seeing the person who assaulted you, the cross-examination can be one of the most intimidating parts of the trial. The defense attorney's job is to make you seem like a less credible witness and cause the jury to question the validity of your testimony. They have various techniques for doing this. The important thing to remember is you are not on trial, even if the defense makes you feel like you are. Whenever possible, give short and direct answers to their questions. If you feel they are trying to confuse you or trip you up, ask them to clarify the question. It's common for the defense attorney to home in on very specific details and ask questions about things they think you might feel guilty about. For example, they might ask how many alcoholic drinks you had or if you went on a date with the person after the assault. Talk to the prosecuting attorney before the trial about any concerns you might have.

When you're being cross-examined, do your best to be yourself. The calmer and more centered you can be, the more you can manage the stress and anxiety you feel. If that's not possible, it's okay. Many survivors have strong emotions when they're on the stand, and there's nothing wrong with crying or asking to take a break. More advice regarding cross-examination from both prosecution and civil attorneys is presented at the end of this chapter.

SUPPORT FROM SURVIVORS: ENCOURAGEMENT AS YOU PREPARE TO TESTIFY

Testifying in court is something that very few survivors of sexual assault have a chance to do. This can make it really hard to find people to connect with who have gone through this experience.

Here are some words of encouragement from those who have gone to court.

"You are even stronger than you know."
"This won't be easy, but that doesn't mean that it isn't the right thing to do."
"This is a situation that none of us wanted to be in. You are incredibly brave and resilient for fighting to be here. No one can take that away from you."
"You know the truth. This is your moment to tell the world that truth."
"This is about you. This is about your journey, your healing, and the justice you deserve. Believe in yourself because all of us survivors believe in you."

EXPERT CONTRIBUTION: PREPARING TO TESTIFY AND PLEA BARGAINS
Brandan Borgos, Esq.

Facing the prospect of testifying after experiencing sexual assault can be an incredibly challenging and emotional journey. As a survivor, it's essential to remember you have a voice, rights, and a support system to help you navigate the legal process. This section aims to provide you with practical steps and heartfelt advice to help you prepare for testifying and to remind you that you are not alone in this journey.

Seeking support and building a support system. Seeking support is crucial during this difficult time. Reach out to trusted friends, family, therapists, or support groups who can provide a listening ear, understanding, and empathy. They can be a source of comfort as you navigate the path ahead. Remember, their support is invaluable and can help you cope with the emotional toll of the trial.

Understanding the legal process. It's important to know that many cases do not proceed without the victim's involvement, and many may never get to the point where you are required to testify at a trial in front of a jury. Even if the case does proceed, your assailant may end up pleading guilty to a different crime. This is called plea bargaining, and is commonplace. Although, according to the Bureau of Justice Statistics (BJS) and the National Center for State Courts, approximately 90 percent of state-level felony convictions are the result of guilty pleas rather than trials, it is unclear how many of these guilty pleas are specifically related to sexual assault cases.[35,36] While your victim impact statement will be considered for the terms of a plea bargain and during sentencing if your assailant gets convicted, you may still want to fully prepare yourself to testify if the case goes to trial.

Plea bargaining is complex and often controversial, especially if you are seeking justice and validation through a trial. It is difficult to not focus on the outcome in these circumstances given these statistics and the realities of how evidence is handled and how jurors interpret it. The outcome is often out of your control, so remember what is in your control, like understanding the legal process, preparing to testify, and leaning on your support systems. This will help ease some of the difficulties and challenges inherent in dealing with our criminal justice system and help to alleviate some of the associated anxiety.

Consult with your attorney, if you have retained one, or your victim advocate to gain clarity on the steps involved in the trial and what to expect. Even the state's attorney may be of assistance, but the benefit of having your own attorney as a guide, even though they won't be appearing in your case, may help you through the process. They can answer any questions you may have and ensure you are well informed and prepared. If you testify, you will be asked questions in direct and cross-examination format and can expand on the following information.

Testifying in general. Remember that testifying in a criminal trial can be a challenging experience, but with the help of a support system and by staying truthful and consistent, you can give strong and credible testimony in court.

When testifying in court, maintain good eye contact and address your answers to the person who asked the question. In most cases, this will be the state's attorney, the prosecutor, or defense attorney who is questioning you. It can be helpful to make brief eye contact with the jurors as well, as they are the ones who will be making the final decision in the case. However, you should primarily focus on the person who asked the question and answer their questions directly and honestly. Always address the judge as "Your Honor" and dress appropriately for court (usually business is best or business casual at a minimum).

If you are feeling nervous or uncomfortable, you can focus on a spot on the wall or a neutral object in the courtroom to help you stay calm and centered. Just remember to periodically make eye contact with the person who asked the question.

Direct examination. During direct examination, the attorney for the state will ask questions to present your experience and establish important facts. This is your opportunity to share your experience in a supportive and controlled environment. Here are some key points to remember:

1. Review your notes: Refer to the notes or any testimony you provided, documenting the assault's details. Familiarize yourself

with the sequence of events, emotions you experienced, and any relevant physical or sensory details. This will help you recall the information during the examination.

2. Speak at your own pace: Take your time when answering questions. Speak clearly and confidently, but don't feel rushed. It's okay to pause and gather your thoughts before responding. Remember, the court and jury want to hear your authentic testimony, so express yourself in your own words.

3. Be truthful and consistent: Your credibility is crucial during the direct examination. Answer questions truthfully, to the best of your ability. If you don't remember specific details or dates, absolutely say so. Consistency in your testimony is important, so try to provide a coherent and accurate account of the events. The state's attorney can refresh your recollection with your prior provided statements if you're having difficulty remembering.

Cross-examination. Cross-examination can be a challenging part of the process, as the defense attorney will ask you questions intended to challenge your credibility or poke holes in your testimony. Here are some strategies to navigate this phase:

1. Stay composed and focused: The defense attorney may use aggressive or intimidating tactics during cross-examination. Remember to stay composed, maintain eye contact with the questioner, and focus on your attorney or a supportive person in the courtroom when needed. Take deep breaths to help calm your nerves.

2. Listen carefully and pause if necessary: Pay close attention to each question asked during cross-examination. Take a moment

to reflect on the question and understand its intent before responding. If you need clarification, kindly ask the attorney to repeat or rephrase the question. Don't be afraid to ask for a break if you feel overwhelmed or emotionally taxed.

3. Stick to the truth and your personal experience: During cross-examination, the defense attorney may attempt to discredit or confuse you. Stay firm in your truth, and rely on your own recollection of events. If you're unsure about a question, it's okay to say, "I don't know" or "I don't remember." Avoid speculating or guessing in your responses.

4. Be mindful of traps and leading questions: The defense attorney might ask leading questions that attempt to put words in your mouth or elicit a specific response. Stay cautious and answer truthfully based on your own experience. If a question is unclear or seems misleading, ask for clarification, or ask to have the question rephrased.

Remember, the state's attorney will be present to guide you and protect the state's interests in obtaining a conviction throughout the questioning process. They will object to improper or unfair questioning techniques when necessary. Trust in their expertise and rely on their advice to navigate through direct and cross-examination with confidence. After cross-examination, they can visit topics that came up during redirect examination, and the defense attorney will have an opportunity to follow up during another cross-examination, usually referred to as re-cross.

Sharing concerns with your attorney. If you are lucky enough to afford your own attorney, remember they are there to guide you through the legal process, protect your rights, and address your concerns. Openly communicate with them about any apprehensions, fears, or questions you may have about testifying. They have experience navigating these sensitive situations and will work with you to find the best approach to support you through the process.

Prioritizing self-care and mental well-being. Preparing to testify can be emotionally draining, and it's crucial to prioritize self-care. Engage in activities that promote mental well-being, such as mindfulness, meditation, or yoga. Take moments to reflect, process your emotions, and practice self-compassion. Allow yourself the time and space needed to heal and recharge during this challenging period.

Sharing your truth with courage. When you take the stand, remember that your testimony is a powerful tool in seeking justice. Your truth matters, and your courageous words can make a significant impact. Testify truthfully, recounting your experience to the best of your ability. Your honesty and authenticity will strengthen the case and help shed light on the truth.

Embracing your rights and dignity. As a survivor of sexual assault, you possess certain rights that should be respected and honored throughout the legal process. These rights include privacy, dignity, and respect. If you have any questions about your rights, don't hesitate to consult your attorney or victim advocate, who can provide guidance and ensure your rights are upheld.

Remember: You are not alone on this journey. Reach out to your support system, lean on them for strength, and never underestimate your resilience. The road ahead may be challenging, but with each step, you are reclaiming your power and standing up for justice. Trust yourself, embrace the support available to you, and know that your voice matters. You have the strength to testify, and your courage will contribute to a system that strives to protect survivors and hold offenders accountable.[37,38]

EXPERT CONTRIBUTION: ADVICE FROM THE PROSECUTION

Kathryn Marsh, Esq., and Melissa Hoppmeyer, Esq.

We're just going to state the obvious. Trial is scary. Testifying is scary. Considering the common defenses used in sexual assault cases, it may seem even scarier. Survivors of sexual assault know their credibility is going to be attacked, and attacked in a way victims of other violent crimes don't experience.

No one asks the victim of a carjacking, "What were you doing driving on that road in the first place?" No one asks the victim of a home invasion, "What did you expect with those types of curtains on display?" And we certainly don't ask a victim of robbery, "Are you sure you didn't consent to being robbed?" However, while these defenses and attacks may seem scary—being forewarned is being forearmed and knowing what to expect may help a survivor stay calm in the courtroom.

Timelines

We have all heard of the "right to a speedy trial," but survivors need to understand that the right to a speedy trial is a right held by the accused, not the prosecution or the victim. Sexual assault trials rarely go to trial on the first scheduled trial date. Prosecutors should do everything they can to help make that happen, but there is a plethora of reasons that often cause delays. These reasons may include: DNA testing still outstanding, unavailability of witnesses, attorneys stuck in other trials that didn't end in time, and court closures, just to name a few. The important thing to know as a survivor is that delays and postponements do not mean that the case is weak or is less likely to go to trial. Unfortunately, delays are a common side effect of overcrowded criminal dockets.

Prior Behavior of the Victim

Victim survivors are often worried about their past behaviors being used against them. This thought process comes from the rape myth that only the most innocent of people can actually be raped, or that the victim must have acted in a certain way to make the accused rape them. Fortunately, states have seen past this common rape myth and most have "rape shield laws." These laws prevent the defense from asking the victim about their prior sexual history or reputation. There are very limited exceptions to rape shield laws, and they generally center around evidentiary issues. For example, someone else's DNA is recovered during a sexual assault. In this case, the victim may be asked about this specific prior sexual experience. This is not something a victim survivor should be worried about. Survivors are allowed to have consensual sex with whomever they choose, and it does not change that the accused sexually assaulted them. The defense may also be able to question the victim survivor if there was a prior consensual sexual relationship between the victim and the accused. In order to ask any questions that would generally be prevented by rape shield laws, the defense must file a motion in advance, and the court will conduct a hearing on the record and provide a ruling on what will or will not be allowed to be asked. The prosecutor will have this ruling before the victim survivor takes the stand and should discuss the parameters with the victim survivor so they are not surprised on the stand.

Cross-Examination

Despite what is commonly depicted in movies or TV shows, rarely does a defense attorney yell or aggressively attack survivors of sexual assault in front of a jury. Instead, there are generally several common forms of attack.

THE YES TRAIN

Defense counsel will attempt to get victim survivors on the yes train, asking questions to have the victim survivor answer yes over and over again and then slip in a question in hope that the victim will answer yes to that question. For example:

a. You went out with friends on January 1, didn't you? Yes.

b. You were all out having a good time, drinking and dancing, correct? Yes.

c. You danced with my client, Mr. Smith? Yes.

d. And at this point in the night, you and Mr. Smith were having a good time, right? Yes.

e. You didn't feel you should drive home on your own, is that correct? Yes.

f. And you were able to make that decision, weren't you? Yes.

g. Mr. Smith offered to give you a ride, didn't he? Yes.

h. And you accepted that ride? Yes.

i. You were able to make that decision, weren't you? Yes.

j. When you got to the house you let Mr. Smith inside, correct? Yes.

k. You told him he could spend the night? Yes.

l. You were able to make that decision on your own? Yes.

m. And then the two of you had sex—

This is where the defense attorney wants the victim survivor to answer yes. The yes implies it was consensual, and victims have been told over and over again to answer questions honestly, and so even though the act was rape and not consensual sex, a victim survivor will often answer yes. The important consideration here is for victims to take their time, listen to the entire question, and answer the question honestly. Just because a question is couched in a yes or no format doesn't mean that's how the victim has to answer. For example: "And then the two of you had sex, correct?" Answer: "No, that's not what happened."

If the defense attorney doesn't allow a victim survivor to explain exactly what happened, the prosecutor will have the opportunity to clarify what happened on redirect. Redirect happens after the defense attorney questions or cross-examines a witness and is allowed for the prosecutor to clarify any issues that arose during cross-examination.

INCONSISTENCIES

Another common tactic is to question survivors about any inconsistencies they may have made in multiple statements. It is important to remember that inconsistencies do not equal lies. If a person has been in a car accident they may be questioned by EMS, police, emergency room medical providers, family members, and loved ones. Depending on the specific questions asked, when the questions were asked, and the relationship the person has with the person asking the questions, there will be differences in answers. These differences don't mean the car accident never happened, it just demonstrates that the person answering the questions is human. A victim survivor should not panic about inconsistencies. A well-prepared prosecutor will be able to review this information with the victim survivor ahead of time and have experts, often psychology experts, available to explain to a judge or jury why inconsistencies happen.

COLLATERAL ISSUES

Another common defense tactic for cross-examination is to ask victim survivors about collateral issues, something that doesn't really have anything to do with the sexual assault, but that the defense attorney wants to imply means the victim isn't telling the truth. This is often done to try to exploit the rape myth that a victim of sexual assault must react in a certain way. Therefore, if the victim survivor is not hiding in their room for days or weeks afterward, they must be lying. These types of questions may include: You went to school/work the next day? You went out with friends? You got your nails done? You posted on social media and never mentioned the rape? You didn't get medical treatment? etc. Again, while these questions are hurtful, it is important to remember that the prosecutor has the opportunity for redirect. Redirect questions may include: Did you want anyone at work or school to know what had just happened to you? The next morning, did you even know how you wanted to handle the rape? Did you want to have to talk to strangers about the sexual assault? Why did you get your nails done? Why didn't you post about the sexual assault on social media? The honest answers to these questions help in explaining the trauma and the thought process of the victim survivor in the immediate aftermath of the sexual assault. And again, well-prepared prosecutors will have experts ready to testify to explain how sexual assault trauma impacts the brain, explain that there is no one way to be a victim, and explain that the sexual assault doesn't have to define each and every action of the victim survivor from that point forward.

Practice

New experiences are easier to face and navigate when we know what to expect. Prior to trial, a victim survivor can and should ask their prosecutor to practice a cross-examination with them. They can even ask to practice in a courtroom. One of the scariest walks someone takes is the walk to the witness box, and just being able to practice that and get an idea of what you will see and hear from the witness box can go a long way to make the scary process of a trial a little easier to handle.

EXPERT CONTRIBUTION: STAGES OF THE CIVIL JUSTICE SYSTEM

Ryan Krupp, Esq.

It is important to note that while criminal justice seeks to provide justice in the form of punishment, it rarely provides any relief for the victim. Legislatures and courts alike have often left that job to the civil court system. Some criminal cases come with mandatory restitution. Nevertheless, in cases of one individual against another, sometimes there is no restitution other than that which can be recovered through an action for negligence where there is an underlying organization or an insurance company that insures for the crime. Due to heightened awareness about systemic sexual assault through organizations, those organizations are increasingly protecting themselves with insurance that would purport to insure victims for the abuse that they have faced, particularly when there is an underlying organization or business involved. This is making access to justice through the civil courts more accessible and practical for victims. Here we will analyze some of the stages of the civil court system and discuss some of the similarities and differences between the civil and criminal courts as described above.

1. Investigative Stage

The investigative stage of the civil justice system is identical to the criminal justice system in that it starts with an investigative agency, usually the police. In some cases, there is a complete overlap of the timeline of the criminal justice system and the civil justice system. This is due to the fact that although many sexual assault–related crimes carry a lengthy statute of limitations (especially those involving children), the statute of limitations for civil cases is often ruthless among states. For the most part the issue is getting worse for victims, rather than better. Many state legislatures ignore the needs of victims and push for reduction of statutes of limitations for the filing of civil cases. Many have two-year statutes of limitations for all civil cases, and some states even have a ruthless one-year timeframe to file a lawsuit with the court to preserve a claim. In an ideal scenario, a victim would be able to cooperate with the criminal investigative agency to come to a full and just resolution to their case prior to deciding whether to engage in the civil process. The reality is that this is rarely a feasible option. Every day that a victim or their family waits to take civil action, the more likely they are to be barred by the system designed to serve them due to the power of corporate interests. For this reason, it is critical for victims and their families to contact a civil lawyer to discuss their options and whether or not they would have a claim, as well as what the statute of limitations would look like in their case.

2. Finding the Right Lawyer

Navigating the civil law process is difficult. In truth, it is far too complex for a victim to navigate alone absent extensive civil law experience. Most civil lawyers have a difficult enough time dealing with all of the moving parts and rules of civil procedure. Combine that with extra rules and laws such as rape shield statutes, questions regarding statements of minors, and civilly prosecuting a perpetrator who may be simultaneously charged in criminal court, and you will see that it is necessary to find the right lawyer.

If possible, it is recommended to contact a civil lawyer who has been through the process of representing victims of sexual assault within the last several years. As a rule of thumb, it is generally the case that the personal injury lawyers you see touted on billboards and daytime TV ads do not have someone who specializes in that field. More specialized areas of law such as sexual assault litigation, products liability, and medical malpractice are often handled by small and mid-sized litigation firms. This is not to say that a larger firm will not have someone specifically dedicated to the practice of victim litigation; rather it is an encouragement to interview several different attorneys until you find one that you know has done the job successfully before and knows what pitfalls to avoid and how to last the course of a tricky civil field.

The next thing to consider is that almost all sexual assault cases could be a civil case. For instance, probably all states have civil assault and battery charges that can be filed. Similarly, all states have some form of civil negligence law in which a civil cause of action can be filed. Even though a victim likely has a case in which there is clear liability and good evidence, many times it does not meet all the requirements in which a lawyer would get involved in the case. A good civil case has all of the following factors:

Liability—Meaning that there is good evidence that the wrongdoing occurred. This is usually a thorough police report, additional victims, witnesses' DNA evidence, or other indicators that the case can be proven to a jury.

Damages—Civil lawyers use the word "damages" to describe physical and emotional distress. In most sexual assault cases, this is an easy check mark because of the terrible psychological damage that has been done to the victim due to the perpetrator's actions.

Collectability—The unfortunate truth is that the civil justice system cannot make a victim whole again. It cannot undo the terrible damage that has been done. The only restitution that can be given is in the form of financial compensation.

While most victims will be able to identify the first two factors, they should seek a good civil attorney to determine whether the third factor is prevalent, such that a lawyer can take the case forward and get the justice the victims deserve for themselves. In some cases, a victim can clearly identify the existence of the third factor. That does not make speaking to a lawyer any less important. In that case, the victim should be seeking the lawyer that is going to bring them the greatest chance at receiving civil justice and should discuss all of their options and resources.

3. Demand Stage

This is an optional stage of litigation. In some circumstances, an organization or insurance company will allow a victim's lawyer to submit a "demand" to an insurance company prior to filing a civil suit. A victim should *never* submit a demand to an insurance company or organization without talking to a lawyer first. Organizations sometimes flip the narrative on the victims, accusing the victim of extortion and effectively destroying their claim. An experienced attorney will know whether or not a demand is appropriate or whether a suit should be filed first.

4. Filing Stage

Once the time is appropriate, a victim's attorney will file a civil lawsuit. The appropriate time is dependent on a number of factors including the statute of limitations, the status of the victim's medical treatment, and other factors. This is usually the beginning of an inefficient but hopefully effective journey.

5. Discovery Stage

"Discovery" in a civil case usually involves an exchange of questions called "interrogatories" and "requests for production." Usually, it is an extensive period of time in which lawyers exchange information related to the case, lodge objections, and make arguments in court. A victim's attorney will likely provide them updates as the process moves forward, but there is usually little required involvement from the victim.

6. Deposition(s)

A deposition is often defined as "a witness's sworn out-of-court testimony." The deposition typically takes place around a conference table wherein the following people are present: (1) The court reporter, (2) prosecuting attorney, (3) defense attorney, (4) witness/victim. This takes place over an unspecified amount of time, usually from one to three hours. A defense attorney will ask a number of questions that the victim will then be required to answer under oath. The deposition is usually the most difficult part of the process for the victim. It is emotionally draining, and often difficult to endure. It is also likely the most important part of the civil litigation for the attorney. During this stage, the victim often gets the first chance to elaborate on the emotional distress and trauma they have faced at the hands of the perpetrator.

7. Expert Evaluation(s)

During the course of civil litigation, it is not uncommon for an attorney of a victim to recommend that they undergo an independent medical evaluation (IME). This involves one or more meetings with an independent medical professional such as a psychiatrist or psychologist. The medical professional will be able to evaluate all of the victim's medical records, depositions, discovery, and any other relevant documents to reach any necessary expert opinions regarding the psychological effects of the assault.

8. Settlement/Trial

First, it should be considered that a great majority of civil cases that are taken by lawyers are eventually settled before trial. Some of these are settled through the process of mediation. Mediation is a process whereby the parties, which usually include a defense lawyer and an insurance adjuster or corporate representative, sit in one room while the victim/plaintiff sits in another room with their lawyer. The parties generally never interact with each other, but a mediator who is usually a former judge or experienced lawyer goes back and forth between the rooms discussing strengths and weaknesses of the case and exchanging valuations for the potential of settlement. The goal of mediation is to come to an agreement between the parties and avoid trial. Not all cases have a mediation, and not all cases that do go to mediation settle, but it is a good way to engage in productive discussions.

Many victims dread the possibility of a civil trial. The victim may have already been through the criminal justice process and all of the scrutiny associated with it. They may also have been unfortunate to have been through a criminal trial. Often the last thing the victim wants is to have to go through another trial. Luckily, unlike in criminal law, a civil trial for a victim of sexual assault is one of the rarest occurrences in civil law. In a world of settlements, civil trial is increasingly rare. Most civil cases involve car accidents; others involve medical malpractice cases. The reason these trials are so few and far between is because sustainable civil cases of sexual assault are a bigger nightmare for defense attorneys and the companies, organizations, or people that they represent. For the first time, the victim is really in the driver's seat. The case is truly all about the victim; it is their chance to actually get justice. If there is an offer on the table, they have the ability to settle the case or push the defense to the edge of trial.

LET'S CHECK IN

Having a self-care plan in place before the trial starts gives you a safety net and a set of tools you'll be able to rely on when the trial is traumatizing. Survivors experience a wide array of emotions during a trial, and although some of them are challenging, many survivors also report feeling proud, determined, strong, and resilient.

The stage after the trial, while you're waiting for the verdict, can take a very long time because, as mentioned, there's no set time limit given to the jury. Keep nurturing yourself, and recognize the immense bravery you displayed. No matter what the verdict is, you did what you could, and that's something to be celebrated.

CHAPTER 10

The Verdict and Sentencing

After enduring everything involved in the reporting, investigation, and trial, the days leading up to the verdict and sentencing can feel like reaching the top of a mountain you've been climbing for a very long time. Preparing yourself to hear the verdict and sentence can help to reduce your anxiety about what the verdict will be and help you to have realistic expectations.

THE VERDICT

As discussed, in a bench trial the judge decides on the verdict, and in a jury trial, the jury determines the verdict. In both cases the evidence presented by the prosecution is evaluated to decide if the evidence proves the defendant is guilty beyond a reasonable doubt.

Beyond a Reasonable Doubt

As we've discussed, the prosecution must prove, beyond a reasonable doubt, that there are no other reasonable explanations for the evidence that was presented in the courtroom to show the crime occurred.[39]

To prove the defendant's guilt beyond a reasonable doubt, prosecution must prove:

- sexual contact occurred,
- there was not consent,
- and any other facts about the charges that were pressed.

For example, if the charges pressed by prosecution include sexual assault with a deadly weapon, the prosecution has to provide enough evidence to prove that a weapon was used. Your victim advocate or the prosecutor representing your court case will be able to tell you what must be proven in your case.

To determine if the burden of proof was met, the judge or jury will consider the credibility of all witnesses, physical evidence, any potential alibi the defendant may have, and any other factors that were presented in court. The judge or jury will then decide on a verdict.

After the verdict is decided, the court will be called into session for the verdict to be read in court. You can be in the courtroom during the verdict, but you are not required to be present. Make the best decision for your well-being. If you attend, you'll sit in the gallery behind the prosecution with any friends, family, and supporters that you want with you. The bailiff will remind everyone in attendance to maintain their composure during court, which means no loud noises, objecting, or sudden or large movements. The defendant will be asked to stand for the verdict, and the judge or designated jury member will share the verdict for each charge the defendant was charged with.

Whether the verdict is guilty or not guilty, you might experience trauma responses like freezing, wanting to yell or fight, or wanting to run out of the room. Talk to your supports about this ahead of time and let them know what you may need and how they can help you. As the verdict is being read, grounding yourself and taking slow, deep breaths can help you to regulate your nervous system.

Processing a Not Guilty Verdict

While it will not be the outcome you intended or expected, it is possible the person who assaulted you will be found not guilty. Preparing yourself for this outcome can help you better process your reactions to the verdict. If the jury finds the defendant not guilty, it doesn't mean the person who assaulted you is innocent. A not guilty verdict also doesn't mean the judge or jury believes you're lying, or that the assault didn't occur. What it *does* mean is the jury determined there wasn't enough evidence presented in the trial to prove guilt beyond a reasonable doubt. Defense attorneys use strategies that can create doubt and suggest that there could be other explanations for any evidence presented.

Some factors that may contribute to a not guilty verdict include:

- lack of evidence,
- inconsistencies in testimony/decreased credibility of witnesses,
- evidence being thrown out,
- having reasonable doubt.

Try to focus on how taking your assailant to court may at least expose their actions and will discourage them from assaulting more people, and if they do, having your court case on record can help a future victim. Lean on your supports. Let them take care of you and take care of yourself. Rest, cry, go for a run, spend time with people you trust—whatever you need to get through this leg of the journey. Not only did you survive sexual assault, but you also braved the court system, held the perpetrator accountable, advocated for yourself, and persevered. Even if you didn't win the case, the battle you fought can help to win the war.

Processing a Guilty Verdict

A guilty verdict doesn't always provide a sense of closure. It may not even feel like the outcome was a true success, and it might not make you happy. It might and I hope it does, but be prepared for a range of complex emotions. You might feel confused, exhausted, happy, sad, or maybe even guilty about the outcome of sharing what happened. Whether the emotions you experience make sense to you or not, consider getting mental health support from a therapist or support group that can hold a safe space and help you to process what you're feeling. Be intentional about taking care of yourself during this time by practicing self-care activities. (See chapter four to review ways to check in with yourself and understand some of the reactions you're having.)

EXPERT CONTRIBUTION: UNDERSTANDING THE SCOPE OF EMOTIONS OF THE VERDICT
Patricia Bathory, MBA, MACP, CCC

First, it's important to say your healing should not depend on this outcome.

Everyone's reaction is different when the verdict is read. Being sexually assaulted is a traumatic event; going through trial is another trauma on top of that. Sometimes the assault survivor must testify, they may have their personal life exposed, insinuations are made about them. It's not a simple or easy process. It's important to note that the trial may be a retraumatizing event. Retraumatization happens when a trauma survivor is exposed to the people, incidents, or circumstances that replay their original trauma—as if it were occurring again.

This is why it's impossible to predict one's feelings after getting a guilty or not guilty verdict. Some possibilities:

Not Guilty

- Feeling of shame—*I just exposed my whole life for nothing, as no justice was done.*
- Embarrassment—*Will people think I was lying? What about all the insinuations made about me, what if people believe they are true? The defense made me look like a totally different person.*

Guilty

- Validation—You feel like the world agrees that what the perpetrator did was wrong. You feel seen and understood.
- Closure—You feel like this chapter is done, and you can start your healing now.

However, I find that often the feelings that arise after a trial are not as clear-cut as we'd expect (i.e., the ones described above). The feelings that follow can be confusing and overwhelming—likely because of the retraumatizing effect of the trial. I've seen the opposite of the expected play out: not guilty verdicts and survivors, though disappointed, being genuinely glad to have the ending of this chapter. I've also seen guilty verdicts where survivors get overwhelmed by immense anger and hatred when the trial comes to an end because the guilty verdict does not give them back the person they used to be before the crime happened. The guilty verdict does not undo what was done to them.

My suggestion here is to try not to let your healing journey be affected by the trial outcome. Visualize them as two completely separate paths (easier said than done, especially after I mentioned the trial is a retraumatizing event).

Your healing journey is composed of your therapy, your self-care, your unpacking of all the feelings and consequences of the assault in your life. The trial is a legal proceeding whose outcome says nothing about the veracity of the assault or the impact it had on you.

While going through the trial, be kind and generous to yourself, especially if your feelings are all over the place, overwhelmed and undefined. Double up on your therapy sessions if you find them helpful, remember to breathe, and take one step at a time.

THE SENTENCING

The sentence, which is determined by the judge, is meant to be appropriate punishment for the person convicted of the crime. The sentencing process varies depending on the jurisdiction and the type of offense that was committed. It begins when a defendant has been convicted after a trial or when a plea bargain has been reached (for more information on plea bargains see chapter nine). The court gathers and reviews information about the defendant, including their criminal history, background, and circumstances around the crime.

Factors the judge will consider when determining a sentence include:

- the severity of the crime,
- the defendant's criminal history,

- relevant legal statutes,
- any special circumstances,
- and the impact on the victim.

As the victim of the crime, you will have an opportunity to share the impact that the crime has had. (Victim impact statements are covered later in this chapter by Attorney Brandan Borgos.)

There are a variety of sentencing options depending on jurisdiction, but some common ones include:

- Incarceration: Jail or prison time is determined.
- Fines: Monetary penalties that the person who committed the crime must pay within a set timeline.
- Restitution: The judge determines that the person who committed the crime must compensate you for your losses that resulted from the crime.
- Probation: This allows the person who committed the crime to remain living in the community, rather than jail or prison, under certain conditions. They may be expected to have regular check-ins with their probation officer, attend therapy, or be restricted on their travel.
- Community Service: In some cases, the judge may require that the person who committed the crime complete a certain number of hours of service that benefit the community.

A separate sentencing hearing will be held where the prosecution and the defense make arguments for what is an appropriate sentence. This is also when the victim impact statement can be read for the court if you choose to share one. Once the judge has had an opportunity to consider relevant factors, they will announce the sentence and typically share their reasoning about how they determined that sentence.

The sentencing process described is sometimes changed because of legal guidelines, jurisdiction, or the judge's discretion. Ask your victim advocate about how your case may proceed differently than what is summarized here.

EXPERT CONTRIBUTION: WRITING A VICTIM IMPACT STATEMENT
Brandan Borgos, Esq.

Victim impact statement. As a survivor of sexual assault, your victim impact statement is more than just words on paper; it is your powerful opportunity to share the profound impact this traumatic experience has had on your life. The trauma you endured could shatter even the strongest person's sense of safety and security, leaving emotional, physical, and financial scars that can be incredibly challenging to heal. In this statement, you can openly express the pain of those scars, your feelings, thoughts, and the daunting challenges you have faced since the assault happened. Some of these may continue into the future, and this is your chance to remind the court that the event's effects may still be felt long after the incident occurred.

Navigating court procedure: finding support for your journey. Facing the court process as a survivor can be overwhelming, but remember that you don't have to go through it alone. Seek support from a victim advocate volunteer or attorney who can guide you through writing your statement and help you understand what to expect. Resources are often available online or through the government or volunteer networks during criminal proceedings to lessen the added stress. Take advantage of these resources early on to have the support you need.

Sharing your truth: the written and oral statement. Your written statement has the power to immerse the judge in your experience, making it a deeply personal and essential document. Choose the format that feels most comfortable for you, whether it is a chronological account, a personal narrative, or a heartfelt letter addressed directly to the judge. You may also have the option to give an oral statement during sentencing, where you can choose to read your written statement again or possibly present a new one. This provides the judge with an opportunity to hear your voice, feel the emotions in your words, and put a face to the crime's impact. If you wish to speak at the sentencing, reach out to your victim advocate or the prosecuting attorney overseeing the case as soon as possible to prepare for your statement. Working with a therapist on emotional preparation and aftercare is highly recommended.

Writing your victim impact statement: honoring your journey. Crafting your victim impact statement can be a deeply emotional process, so be gentle with yourself and seek support from your therapist and victim advocate if needed. Focus on your unique journey and consider the following points to help prepare your statement:

- Begin the statement by addressing the court/judge respectfully. Use formal language and be mindful of the setting in court.
- Be authentic and reflect on life before the assault and how it has dramatically changed since. This can include your relationships, daily activities, and overall well-being. Comparing the before, after, and now in the following ways can really help the court understand what you have gone through.

- Express any effects the assault had on your emotional (including any triggers you experienced along the way or now that you did not before), financial (like lost work time, medical bills, or ongoing therapy expenses), and social (family, friends, dating, romantic relationships) life. If you feel ready for them, include any hopes for your future you have.
- Find out beforehand if the court restricts the amount of space or the format your statement can take.
- Share your recommendations for the court regarding the sentence.
- Respect your boundaries if there are aspects of the crime or its impact that you are not comfortable sharing, and know that it is entirely acceptable to keep those private.
- Keep it concise because, while it is essential to include significant details about your experience, the points above are most impactful to the case.
- Seek help in proofreading and writing your statement from an advocate, therapist, or counselor, and recognize that it, and even this guide, is not legal advice. Only a licensed attorney who knows the details of the case and your experience can provide that.
- There is often a deadline for submitting a statement, so be sure to do that on time.

Empower your voice: seeking healing and justice. As you prepare for your victim impact statement, remember that you have the right as a survivor to communicate the profound effects of the assault on your life. Whether you choose to present your statement in writing or orally, remember that you are directing your remarks to the judge, not the person who assaulted you.

Prepare for the possibility of strong emotions before, during, or after delivering your statement. If you find yourself unable to complete it, see if the court allows an alternate person to read or finish reading it. If you cannot or do not want to be present at the sentencing hearing, that is completely understandable. In many cases, the victim advocate or the prosecutor will read your statement to the court if you do not want to or can't finish it. Be sure to check in with them before the hearing starts to briefly talk with them about this.

Keep in mind that it is the process, your intentions, the help you receive along the way, and the work you do, not the outcome, that will determine the majority and direction of your healing path. Even with a little bit of help and support, you can write a statement that is deeply meaningful to you and will put a face and a real person before the judge.

If you decide not to write a statement, that is okay, too. Just know it is an option and one of the things you have control over in a process that can largely feel out of your hands.

SUPPORT FROM SURVIVORS: WHAT ARE SOME WAYS YOUR SEXUAL ASSAULT IMPACTED YOUR LIFE?

When thinking about your victim impact statement, consider the wide range of ways that your assault may have changed your life. Other survivors share ways that their assault changed their life.

"It changed my career course after I wasn't able to keep working due to the PTSD symptoms I had."

"I dropped out of school in order to address my mental health."

"I have been in weekly therapy now for three years, all related to the impacts of being assaulted."

"The harassment got so bad that I had to change jobs because of them."

"I actually haven't been intimate or romantic with anyone since the assault."

"I no longer enjoyed going dancing or hanging out with my friends."

"I developed an eating disorder that I am still working through."

"I turned to substances to cope and had to receive treatment. I was able to work through it, but I felt like I didn't understand my addiction and how it related to my trauma for a very long time."

LET'S CHECK IN

Waiting for the verdict and sentencing can take a lot of time and mental space, and when the trial is over, you might feel unsure about what to do next and how to move forward. It's helpful to have therapy services, not only about the assault, but also about your reporting and court experience and the aftermath of the trial. For example, it can feel isolating and upsetting to see your support, family, and friends return to "life as normal" when you're still processing the crime and the trial.

Now that the trial is over, try to think about all the wonderful things you want to do with your time and energy, including your own healing. You may find that you want to rediscover what brings you joy and what makes life meaningful for you. As you follow your path to healing, celebrate the courage and resiliency that you've shown and all the ways that you've become even stronger.

Part III provided information and guidance regarding what to expect from the legal process. Whether or not your case made it to court, we all will continue to move forward with our healing. Part IV will offer a variety of options for your healing journey.

Part IV

CHAPTER 11

The Healing Journey

A hard truth is that experiencing sexual assault can have long-term effects on your mental and physical health, your relationships with others, and the relationship you have with yourself. In this chapter, I'll broadly share information that addresses various diagnoses, treatment options, and things to consider when designing your own healing experience. For detailed information, to get a diagnosis, to learn more about different diagnoses, and to receive treatment, consult a health care professional. For right now, learning about the effects of trauma can give you the ability to better understand your behaviors and mental health, and also to advocate for yourself. It's important to note here that these issues are complicated and to cover them all in depth goes beyond the scope of this book. Understanding the ongoing symptoms and impacts of sexual assault allows us to lead more fulfilling lives by giving us tools to manage those effects. My intention with this chapter is to give you the basic tools to start conversations with your medical and mental health teams and get information to better advocate for yourself if needed. For detailed information regarding any of these diagnoses, symptoms, or treatments, you will need to talk in depth to those teams.

BODY AND BRAIN: WHAT YOU MIGHT EXPERIENCE POST ASSAULT

In the aftermath of sexual assault, either immediately or as time passes, you may experience a wide range of symptoms. You might experience all of these symptoms, none of them, or ones that aren't covered here, because everyone is different. After trauma, some people experience psychological distress and physical symptoms, because the human body's stress response remains activated. The mental and physical effects of trauma can be long-lasting, but with support and work you can move toward healing and recovery.

MINDING YOUR MIND

Because the effects of trauma can be difficult to deal with without appropriate support and professional help, it's essential that you have access to the resources you need and a community that understands and validates your experience. Knowing about the symptoms you may experience after sexual assault, and a little about the diagnoses you might be given before you meet with professionals, can help you to understand what they're saying and prepare you to ask questions about treatment and healing options. The following conditions are common mental health challenges that may arise after assault.

Anxiety and Post-Traumatic Stress Disorder

Feelings of anxiety are a normal part of life. But when anxiety becomes intense and persistent over an extended period of time, it may be an anxiety disorder. Post-traumatic stress disorder (PTSD) in particular is an anxiety disorder that's caused by a traumatic event. Survivors of sexual assault can experience feelings of fear, anxiety, stress, and panic long after their assault occurred; these feelings may become so intense that they interfere with daily activities or your ability to function at home, work, or in your relationships. You might experience flashbacks that make you feel like you're reliving the event in the current moment. You might have nightmares and intrusive thoughts. Other symptoms include hyperarousal, which makes you feel like you're constantly on edge. You may easily become overstimulated and have trouble sleeping. PTSD can also lead to avoidant behaviors like changing your routine to avoid people and places. The people or places might be, or seem to be, directly connected to the assault, like the house or neighborhood where it happened or the place the assaulter works or goes to school. You might also find yourself avoiding people or places that aren't directly connected to your assault. If that happens, it can be helpful to process it with a therapist so you can start to figure out what's causing the fear or anxiety. For example, I'd always felt comfortable at the gym, but after I was assaulted, I felt incredibly vulnerable there. With time and therapy, I realized that I didn't feel safe at the gym because I was assaulted by an athlete, and at the gym I was surrounded by physically fit men.

PTSD manifests differently for each person, but understanding why it's happening can remove the added challenge of not knowing why you're being triggered. If you're experiencing or start to experience PTSD, work with your care team to get support in managing your symptoms, and if one treatment method doesn't work for you, keep trying other treatments until you find one that works. No one should have to live with the everyday impacts of PTSD.

Depression

Classified as a mood disorder, depression is characterized by persistent feelings of sadness and hopelessness. It's a common condition. Each year, more than 18 million adults in the United States are affected,[40] and 11 percent of Americans twelve years and older take antidepressant medication.[41]

It's possible you were struggling with depression even prior to your assault, and many survivors develop real, clinical depression after their assault. If these feelings are new to you and persist for weeks or months and they begin to interfere with your activities at work or home, it is essential you seek out professional help. You can't think your way out of depression and, when clinical, it doesn't pass on its own.

Low Self-Esteem and Self-Worth

Because sexual assault is a trauma where our body is used to inflict harm, it's normal to experience a cascade of confusing feelings during and afterward. Many survivors report feelings of shame and vulnerability and may place blame on themselves or feel guilty, instead of blaming the perpetrator.

Negative perceptions about your self-worth and appearance may create a diminished sense of self, and can sometimes lead to unhealthy choices and behaviors like not taking care of your physical body or health. People may turn to overeating, not eating, substances, not completing hygienic care, unsafe sex practices, or dressing differently than they did before the assault to avoid attention or feel a greater sense of control.

In a perfect world, survivors would receive the support and resources they need, but in the real world, this isn't the case. People who don't have access to these things may, understandably, turn to maladaptive coping skills in order to live with the mental and emotional pain that the trauma caused. It's well known that experiencing sexual assault puts people at an increased risk of developing substance use disorders, including alcohol use disorder.[42] Because alcohol and drugs can temporarily numb the negative and distressing memories associated with the trauma, this support can turn into a habit and without intervention become a long-term dependency.

Survivors may also resort to self-harm or develop an eating disorder as they attempt to deal with the emotional pain. Both men and women who have experienced sexual assault are at an increased risk of developing an eating disorder.[43] A review of college-age men who were sexually assaulted showed a correlation with having eating disorders.[44]

If you engaged in these activities, it can help to acknowledge that you did the best you could with the resources and information you had at the time. If you're using these mechanisms now, we can always start down a path of healing. The first step is building awareness for how we cope, and identifying the coping mechanisms that are causing us harm so we can work toward reducing those behaviors and replacing them with healthier ones, as discussed later in this chapter.

The most important relationship you'll ever have is the one you have with yourself. Taking the time to invest in your own healing will help you with all the other relationships in your life.

GLIMMERS: THE ANTIDOTE TO TRIGGERS

The term "glimmers" was coined by Deb Dana, a licensed clinical social worker specializing in complex trauma and author of *The Polyvagal Theory in Therapy*. Dana defines glimmers as small moments and cues to our nervous system to feel safe or calm. They reduce our emotional distress and help restore our bodies and minds to a healthier state. Glimmers might be random acts of kindness, spending quality time with your pet, or finishing a challenging hike. Knowing our glimmers is just as valuable in our healing process as knowing our triggers. Being aware of our triggers and glimmers can help us to regulate our emotions and PTSD symptoms. We can also intentionally seek out and provide ourselves with the environments and situations that help us feel safe and to thrive.

SUPPORT FROM SURVIVORS: TRIGGERS AND GLIMMERS

What are some of your triggers?

"Playing cards. We were playing cards the night it happened."

"Being around people who are intoxicated."

"People saying sexual things to me."

"The smell of beer."

"Certain colognes."

"Having anyone else sleep in my bed."

"Whenever I hear the song that was playing the night it happened."

"Walking by myself."

"People who have the same hairstyle they did."

What are some of your glimmers?

"Seeing videos of people on social media who are on a similar healing journey to me and are thriving."

"Appreciating art and creative writing."

"Hiking and reaching my destination."

"A warm blanket with tea and a movie."

"Horseback riding by myself on the trail."

"Going for a long run."

"Spending time with my best friend always leaves my heart feeling more full."

"Dancing! Anywhere, even just in my room."

"Watching the sunrise."

"Car rides with loud music I can scream to."

"Baths and warm showers. Water is so calming for me."

"Seeing the people I love smile."

"The sound of waves hitting the shore."

"Learning a new skill."

"Hearing my wife laugh."

EXPERT CONTRIBUTION: MENTAL HEALTH AND SEXUAL ASSAULT

Heather J. Peters, PhD, LP

I was raped when I was twenty-five years old. For a long time, I spoke about the rape as though it was something that happened to someone else. I was very aware that it had happened to me, but there was just no feeling. Then I started having flashbacks. They kind of came over me like a splash of water. I would be terrified. Suddenly I was reliving the rape. Every instant was startling. I wasn't aware of anything around me. I was in a bubble, just kind of floating. And it was scary.[45]

The above experience, shared by an anonymous source, exemplifies one of the four common outcomes or trajectories individuals experience after being exposed to a traumatic incident (Bryant, 2013), such as sexual assault:

1. *Resilience*: relatively stable functioning and few symptoms resulting from the trauma.
2. *Recovery*: initial distress, with reduction in symptoms over time.
3. *Delayed symptoms*: few initial symptoms followed by increasing symptoms over time (as demonstrated in the above quote).
4. *Chronic symptoms*: consistently high trauma-related symptoms that begin soon after the event.

Initial stress reactions that occur shortly after a sexual assault are normal responses to an overwhelming and threatening situation. For some people, however, the response to the sexual assault lasts for more than several days and results in an acute stress disorder. An acute stress disorder is characterized by symptoms that last from three days to one month after the sexual assault.

Symptoms of acute stress disorder fall into five categories: intrusion symptoms; negative mood; dissociative symptoms; avoidance symptoms; and arousal symptoms. In addition to acute stress disorder, sexual assault is associated with increased risk for many psychological disorders. Specifically, individuals who have experienced sexual assault, compared to individuals who have not experienced sexual assault, are at higher risk for generalized anxiety disorder, social anxiety, panic attack, agoraphobia, dysthymia, major depressive disorder, bipolar disorders, bulimia nervosa, obsessive-compulsive disorder, post-traumatic stress disorder (PTSD), and all substance use disorders (see definitions in the table that follows). The following table shows the higher prevalence rates associated with psychological disorders for people who have experienced sexual assault compared to those who have not experienced sexual assault.

Disorder	Lifetime Prevalence Sexual Assault	Lifetime Prevalence No Sexual Assault
Anxiety Disorders	20%	10%
Bipolar Disorder	9%	2%
Depressive Disorders	39%	17%
Eating Disorders	8%	2%
Obsessive-Compulsive Disorder	6%	2%
Post-traumatic Stress Disorder	36%	9%
Substance Use Disorder	19%	9%

(Dworkin, 2020)

As the above table demonstrates, depressive disorders and PTSD appear to be particularly common in people who have experienced sexual assault. PTSD and depressive disorders are highly treatable using short-term cognitive behavioral therapies. Evidence-based treatments for PTSD include cognitive processing therapy (Resick, Monson, and Chard, 2014) and prolonged exposure (Rothbaum, Foa, and Hembree, 2007); evidence-based treatments for depression include cognitive therapy (Beck, Rush, Shaw, and Emery, 1979) and behavioral activation (Lejuez, Hopko, and Hopko, 2001). These treatments are associated with substantial reductions in symptoms within twelve to sixteen sessions and represent efficient and cost-effective strategies. It is important to keep in mind that most individuals who experience trauma recover; they show a significant decrease or full remission in symptoms with time (Santiago et al., 2013).

BRIEF DEFINITIONS OF PSYCHOLOGICAL DISORDERS ASSOCIATED WITH SEXUAL ASSAULT
(adapted from Sue, Sue, Sue, and Sue, 2022)

Acute stress disorder (ASD) is characterized by flashbacks, hyper-vigilance, and avoidance symptoms that last between three days to one month after exposure to a traumatic stressor.

Agoraphobia is an intense fear of being in public places where escape or help may not be readily available.

Bipolar Disorders

- **Bipolar I disorder** is characterized by at least one manic episode (i.e., a distinct period of abnormally and persistently elevated, expansive, or irritable mood and persistently increased activity or energy) that has impaired social or occupational functioning; the person may or may not experience depression or psychotic symptoms.

- **Bipolar II disorder** is characterized by at least one major depressive episode and at least one hypomanic episode (i.e., a milder form of mania involving increased levels of activity and goal directed behaviors combined with an elevated, expansive, or irritable mood).

Bulimia nervosa is an eating disorder in which episodes involving rapid consumption of large quantities of food and a loss of control over eating are followed by purging, excessive exercise, or fasting in an attempt to compensate for binges.

Dysthymia, also known as persistent depressive disorder, is a condition involving chronic depressive symptoms that are present most of the day for more days than not during a two-year period with no more than two months symptom-free.

Generalized anxiety disorder (GAD) is characterized by persistent high levels of anxiety and excessive worry over many life circumstances.

Major depressive disorder (MDD) is a condition diagnosed if someone (without a history of hypomania/mania) experiences a depressive episode involving severe depressive symptoms that have negatively affected functioning most of the day nearly every day for at least two full weeks.

Obsessive-compulsive disorder (OCD) is characterized by intrusive, repetitive anxiety-producing thoughts or a strong need to perform acts to reduce anxiety.

Panic attack is characterized by an episode of intense fear accompanied by symptoms such as a pounding heart, trembling, shortness of breath, and fear of losing control or dying.

Post-traumatic stress disorder (PTSD) is characterized by flashbacks, hypervigilance, avoidance, and other symptoms that last longer than one month and occur as a result of exposure to extreme trauma.

Social anxiety disorder (SAD) is an intense fear of being scrutinized in social or performance situations.

Substance use disorders (SUD) is a condition in which cognitive, behavioral, and physiological symptoms contribute to the continued use of alcohol or drugs despite significant substance-related problems.[46,47,48,49,50,51,52,53]

MENDING YOUR BODY

After an assault, the focus tends to be on the psychological and emotional symptoms you're having, but you may also experience physical effects. When we experience a traumatic event like sexual assault, our body's stress response system becomes activated and releases hormones like cortisol and adrenaline. The effects of these hormones include increased heart rate, increased blood pressure, and tensing of our muscles. In the immediate moment, these responses are normal and help us to survive the trauma. However, over time the chronic activation of these hormones can be toxic to our bodies and lead to systemic health concerns including gastrointestinal disorders, weakened immune functions, sleep disturbances, and more. In addition to the impact of these stress hormones, trauma can affect our eating habits, lead to substance use, and disturb our sleep, which can further impact our physical health.

Our understanding of how trauma impacts our bodies continues to deepen; for example, there is a correlation between adverse childhood experiences (ACEs) and chronic health conditions.[54] What we know now is that there are biological changes that are associated with PTSD, including changes in the limbic system, dysregulation of arousal systems in the body, and changes in cortisol levels.[55]

There are some excellent resources available to better understand the effects of trauma on the body, including the book *The Body Keeps the Score: Brain, Mind, and Body in the Healing of Trauma* by Bessel van der Kolk. This resource has become fundamental for trauma survivors because it explains how unresolved trauma has lasting impacts on our physical body. The book makes connections between trauma and chronic pain, how the ongoing release of stress hormones impacts the brain and mental health, how trauma disrupts neuropathways and how they can be repaired, and even how trauma affects relationships.

Making sure you build your support team to include doctors and other health care professionals who are trauma-informed can help ensure that you receive well-rounded care.

CHECKING IN

Begin to create a healing plan that works well for your indi-vidualized needs if you know what those needs are. Give some thought to these questions and write down your answers if you think it will be helpful in moving forward.

- What are my known triggers?
- What are my known glimmers?
- When I feel stressed, anxious, or triggered, where do I feel those emotions in my body?
- What is one thing I can do today to help myself feel safe?

It sometimes feels like trauma is taking over our entire life, but being a survivor of sexual assault doesn't define us and it doesn't have to limit us. Surviving trauma shows how strong, resilient, and determined we are to heal and grow.

THERAPIES AND PRACTICES FOR HEALING

You already know that for therapy to be effective, you have to work with a therapist whose style works for you. If you haven't started therapy, there are a wide variety of therapeutic approaches. The following are some more common ones used for people who have experienced sexual assault:

Trauma-Focused Cognitive Behavioral Therapy (TF-CBT): This type of therapy helps people to identify and reframe negative or harmful thought patterns and change trauma-related behaviors. For example, trauma can lead to repeated thoughts of self-blame, and TF-CBT can help to challenge and change those destructive thought patterns that we might not even realize that we have. It also teaches skills in regulating emotions and identifying and learning coping skills.

Eye Movement Desensitization and Reprocessing (EMDR): This is a specialized therapy designed to process traumatic memories through bilateral stimulation (such as your eyes moving back and forth following an object or tapping your shoulders in an alternating pattern). This bilateral stimulation is done while focusing on distressing memories and can help to reduce the emotional intensity of those memories over time.

Dialectical Behavior Therapy (DBT): This therapy incorporates elements of cognitive behavioral therapy (CBT) with mindfulness practices. It can be altered specifically for those who have PTSD, and it has been found to be especially promising for PTSD from childhood sexual abuse.[56] An example of a DBT exercise is increasing mindfulness or awareness about the emotions you're feeling in different situations.

Psychodynamic Therapy: Psychodynamic therapy focuses on exploring unconscious processes that may influence current emotions and behaviors. It can improve self-esteem and increase awareness and ability to understand reactions to trauma.[57]

Somatic Experiencing: Somatic therapy uses a body-focused approach. This therapy supports the survivor in focusing on the physical sensations they feel after trauma and stressful situations.[58] Trauma can be stored in the body and manifest as tension or pain. After experiencing sexual assault, survivors may have physical effects that can become chronic without intervention.

Acceptance and Commitment Therapy (ACT): ACT focuses on acceptance and mindfulness strategies to help survivors live more fully in the present and pursue meaningful life goals instead of focusing on reducing symptoms.[59] Instead of reviewing behaviors and thought patterns that you want to change, with this practice you focus on future goals and how to reach them.

Art Therapy: Engaging in art therapy can be a powerful tool in healing, self-discovery, and expression. A big value is that it provides a creative and nonverbal way for survivors to express their emotions and process the trauma. Children who have been sexually assaulted might better be able to express themselves in this therapy form.

Drug and Addiction Counseling: Drug and addiction counseling can be crucial for sexual assault survivors who turn to substances as a way to cope with the trauma and its emotional aftermath. Sexual assault can lead to using drugs or alcohol to numb emotions or forget the trauma, but relying on substances to cope can increase emotional and psychological challenges and lead to addiction. This type of counseling helps survivors to address maladaptive coping mechanisms, learn healthier coping skills, get resources for mental health and addiction, identify triggers, and provide support to prevent relapse.

Support Groups: Support groups and group therapy offer a welcoming and validating environment for sexual assault survivors. Being with people who can offer empathy and validation helps us to feel less alone in our experiences, and we can also learn a lot from one another. Someone in the group might have tried a new therapy or might know of a helpful resource that others in the group did not know about. Participating in support groups helps survivors to build connections with people they can process the trauma with.

Joining a group led by a therapist who is trained and experienced in trauma and sexual assault is important because they can structure the environment and interaction so that survivors feel safe.

NEW INNOVATIONS IN THERAPY

If time has passed since your assault and the types of therapies listed previously haven't been effective for you, there are some new, research-based approaches that involve external stimuli to help address trauma symptoms. These treatments are not yet widely accessible, but if you're interested in them, discuss the possibility with your current therapist or doctor.

- **Transcranial Magnetic Stimulation (TMS):** TMS is a non-invasive medical procedure where electromagnetic coils are used to create magnetic fields that pass through the skull and stimulate specific brain regions. It's being used for a wide variety of neurological and psychiatric diagnoses, including PTSD.
- **Neurofeedback Therapy:** Neurofeedback therapy is a relatively new and promising approach to treat symptoms of PTSD. Neurofeedback therapy is a non-invasive approach, where sensors are placed on the person's scalp to monitor their brainwave patterns and provide real-time feedback on brain activity. With this feedback, trained professionals can help each individual learn how to self-regulate their brain activity.

MINDFULNESS AND AFFIRMATIONS

Mindfulness is a practice that involves paying attention to the present moment without feeling judgment for the thoughts, emotions, or sensations that you're experiencing. Research has proven that practicing mindfulness is a very effective tool for improving and maintaining mental health.

Benefits of mindfulness include:

- increased emotional regulation,
- decreased reactivity to things happening around us,
- increased relationship satisfaction,
- increased empathy,
- decreased stress and anxiety.[60]

Mindfulness can be developed many different ways, including through meditation, body scans, breathing exercises, and mindful movement practices such as yoga.

Examples of structured mindfulness-based practices include Mindfulness-Based Stress Reduction (MBSR) and Mindfulness-Based Cognitive Therapy (MBCT). Both MBSR and MBCT are structured programs where you attend sessions led by a certified instructor to develop mindfulness skills. The goal of these programs is to help people develop a practice to increase their resilience, awareness of their emotions, and become more aware of their body sensations. MBSR tends to focus more on general mindfulness, anxiety disorders, and stress, compared to MBCT, which is designed for those with recurrent depression. Both are very beneficial to survivors of assault.

Affirmations are statements that are repeated regularly with the intention of setting a positive belief about the world around us, our experiences, and ourselves. They can increase self-confidence, improve resilience, encourage positive habits, and create a sense of gratitude.

Some examples of affirmations include:

- "I believe in myself and my abilities."
- "I am worthy of happiness and healing."
- "I love and accept myself."

- "I am proud of who I am and all that I have survived."
- "I trust that I can handle whatever comes my way."
- "I am deserving of all good things that come my way."
- "I am constantly growing and learning."

Some of these might feel uncomfortable at first. We may not feel like these statements are true about ourselves after experiencing trauma, but they absolutely are. You deserve good things. You are strong. You are growing, healing, and are worthy of love. The person who harmed you might have made you question these things, but part of getting our power back is reclaiming these beliefs and knowing them to be true.

Both affirmations and mindfulness must be practiced consistently before they begin to show their benefits, so find ways to incorporate them into your day. You can set timers or timed notifications on your phone to remind you to practice or post notes around your home.

SUPPORT FROM SURVIVORS: WHAT ARE YOUR AFFIRMATIONS?

"I am a survivor."

"I am not defined by what happened to me, I define my own identity."

"I am healing at my own pace, and every step is a victory."

"This is my body."

"My voice deserves to be heard."

"I am in control of my life and I choose to move forward, one step at a time."

"I embrace intimacy in my life on my terms."

"I will accept help and healing."

"I am resilient."

"I will honor myself."

"I deserve love."

"This is my body. This is my life."

"I have choice. I have power."

"My PTSD is not who I am."

"My trauma response doesn't define me, I define me."

NURTURING YOUR BODY

Moving your body can be a healing and powerful practice to incorporate into your routine because it can:

- Release stress, relax you, and lead to a sense of relief.
- Empower you by showing control of your body.
- Help you feel proud of your body again for being strong and for what it allows you to do.
- Be a safe way to remember that we have personal space and ownership over our body.
- Release endorphins, which can naturally make your mood brighter and improve your self-esteem.
- Be an opportunity to build relationships and connections, which is an important part of the healing process.

To move and connect to your body, consider trying:

- Yoga
- Weightlifting
- Walking
- Group fitness classes
- Fitness training
- Running

- Biking
- Hiking
- Massage
- Acupuncture

- Horseback riding
- Doing outdoor chores
- Swimming
- Dancing

Variety can make the healing journey more enjoyable, but be sure to choose exercise that feels safe to you. Start slowly, and listen to your body throughout the process, and you may discover that you like movement more than you thought you would. Before beginning any new physical routine, touch base with your health care provider to ensure there are no risks to your health and safety.

Nutrition

Nutrition plays a significant role in physical recovery and emotional well-being, but trauma can impact our relationship with food and our body image, which can make it challenging to meet nutritional needs. Finding a way to take care of your nutritional needs will increase energy, reduce stress, and improve your gut health. Research studies show that our gut microbiome (the bacteria in your digestive system) plays an important role with anxiety disorders[61] because the relationship between stress and changes in the gut's microbiome affect our digestion and ability to absorb nutrients. In addition to supporting our recovery, eating healthy foods is a wonderful way to care for and feel more love for our bodies.

Recommendations for taking steps toward healthier nutritional practices:

- Plan meals for the week ahead.
- Incorporate more fresh vegetables and fruits.

- Find recipes that are simple to make.
- Meet with a registered dietitian.

For more details on our relationship with food and how a dietitian can be a beneficial asset to your health care team, see the Q & A with a Dietitian by Angela Goens on page 113.

EXPERT CONTRIBUTION: BENEFITS OF FINDING A FITNESS COMMUNITY

Cate Schultz, BA, Certified Therapeutic Coach, CrossFit Instructor, Yoga Instructor, Circle Facilitator

Feeling strong is a muscle we have to build literally and figuratively. We start by showing up and lifting weights, and pretty soon, we see our physical body experience a new strength. The next thing we know, that physical strength spreads into our mentality and emotional well-being. When you can choose to show up for yourself and pick up those weights, you are proving to yourself over and over again, you are enough.

Sometimes we also need reminders about how strong we are from those around us. Let your community reinforce how amazing you are. Find a fitness community built around consistency and support. When you enter a gym that portrays the importance of community, ask them how they define community and then make sure it aligns with what you want out of a community before signing up.

When you can care for yourself through exercise, it builds confidence and self-esteem. When you can care for yourself through exercise alongside a community of people, the impact is life-changing!

OTHER WAYS TO FIND HEALING

There are many other healing practices that focus on restoring balance and harmony within yourself and with your community. For example, some healing practices incorporate a holistic approach, based on values unique to particular cultures. Our culture influences how our trauma affects us and how we choose to heal. As we think about how we want to heal, it can be helpful to keep our unique culture, religious beliefs, and communities in mind. Some examples include:

- community support,
- ceremonial practices and rituals,
- connections to nature,
- oral traditions and storytelling,
- herbal medicines,
- spiritual guidance and prayer.

EXPERT CONTRIBUTION: PETS AND TRAUMA
Ruth Goins, DVM

People who have pets know how comforting they can be in times of distress. It seems like animals "just know" when we're upset and provide us with emotional support in the form of cuddles, purring, or the opportunity to get out of the house for a walk. Pets have been proven to fill the gap left by busy family members during times of loss, since they're always around us. While there is scant research on the effects of emotional support animals, there is undeniable anecdotal evidence that pets can help those healing from trauma.

Animals can help facilitate trauma processing by helping you establish secure attachments. This lessens negative effects on the nervous system that may be present due to attachment insecurity. A pet can be a stand-in for human attachment, but also serve as a conduit for broadening relationships and socialization opportunities. During therapy sessions, animals can provide a grounding presence and a way for people to proceed with trauma therapy. In addition, animals can provide pleasant sensory stimulation and induce the release of oxytocin, both of which can enhance a healing environment.

Although animals can be a huge benefit when healing from trauma, there are certain precautions to consider if you're thinking of adopting an emotional support animal. First, animals require attention and care, which costs time and money. Unfortunately, not everyone's lifestyle or finances are aligned with these expenses, so it's important to be realistic about whether adopting an animal will be as good for them as it may be for you. Additionally, the loss of a beloved animal is often incredibly painful and can be traumatic as well. A support system for pet loss should be in place if additional losses or traumas could significantly stall or set back your healing. Finally, if you become emotionally dependent on a pet, it can limit your progress in healing.

When pursued thoughtfully, having an emotional support animal can be a cornerstone of trauma healing. However, it is also important to continue to pursue evidence-based therapies and medications.[62,63,64,65]

WORKING ON OUR RELATIONSHIPS

Trauma survivors may have ongoing feelings of fear, mistrust, and vulnerability and struggle with communication, setting boundaries, and self-esteem. Unfortunately, these feelings and struggles can make you want to avoid developing relationships and starting new ones. It can be motivating to know that relationships can give you the incentive to stay on the healing journey and to pursue healthy interests including recreation, sports, and hobbies. The people we have strong relationships with also provide emotional support, help us to reduce stress, and encourage us to lead more fulfilling lives.

Platonic Relationships

Our friends offer companionship, community, and support, so building or rebuilding friendships after assault is essential. If it feels intimidating or you don't know where to start, here are some suggestions:

- Work with a therapist or counselor who specializes in trauma for guidance about safe ways to make connections and to work on coping skills to manage healthy relationships.
- Find comfortable and safe environments to meet supportive people. These can be places you already go (a church, fitness center, farmers market) or someplace new (like a store that hosts book clubs or a restaurant that offers a cooking class). Other ways to meet supportive people are through group therapy or support groups.
- Communicate your boundaries and limits. For example, think about the boundaries you have around disclosing your trauma or going to events where people may be intoxicated. Make sure to share those boundaries and know how to spot when those boundaries are being violated.
- Practice self-care and be kind to yourself. Relationships are a wonderful component to living a full life, but conflicts will come up, and making sure to take care of your physical and mental health will be important to maintaining healthy relationships.

This may mean taking your time to build relationships, being patient with yourself, and opening up gradually to new people. Remember, you don't owe anyone your story.

Romantic and Intimate Relationships

Navigating sexuality and relationships after being sexually assaulted is one of the biggest challenges that many survivors face. The long-lasting impacts can include decreased interest in sex (hyposexuality), increased interest in sex (hypersexuality), pain during intercourse, and difficulties with arousal or orgasm. Survivors may also struggle with trust, intimacy, and establishing healthy boundaries in intimate relationships.

These challenges can evoke many emotions, including shame, fear, and guilt. If you're experiencing these physical issues or negative emotions about them, it will be very difficult to work through them on your own, so this is another area where getting professional support can make a tremendous difference. From what others have shared with me, it's well worth the effort—working through these challenges and having a healthy and loving relationship can be one of the most rewarding parts of a survivor's journey.

The suggestions for building platonic relationships apply to dating as well. But some additional things to keep in mind include:

- Date on your terms. Suggest meeting in public places, plan the dates yourself, and tell a friend the date's name and when and where you're going.
- Decide what you're comfortable with—or not—ahead of time and let your date know. You might express that you don't want to have physical contact or that you want the date to be in a public setting. You can also feel more prepared for the date if

you decide ahead of time what, if anything, you want to share about your assault, keeping in mind that you don't have to share anything at all. (Review disclosing on page 93.)

- Notice their actions and words. For example, if they treat the restaurant staff disrespectfully, defend a celebrity who's accused of sexual assault, or make victim-blaming statements, they're giving you good reasons to question whether you want to spend more time with them.
- Acknowledge and celebrate the wins! Even the small victories that show progress in your healing and dating are worth celebrating. For example, if in the past you've had a hard time setting boundaries, choosing not to go on a second date with someone you didn't feel comfortable with is a huge victory.

Parenting

Parenting after sexual assault can present unique challenges, but with self-compassion and the right support, you can navigate parenthood and create or maintain a nurturing environment for your children. As a parent, or soon-to-be parent, seek support from professionals who can provide resources and a safe space to process emotions and triggers. Know that it's okay and healthy to set boundaries to help manage your energy and emotions while providing a sense of security for your children. Build a network with friends, family, and other survivors who can help by providing support such as bringing meals when you're having a particularly challenging day. You may also want to consider seeking counseling for your children to support their emotional well-being.

As you learn how to navigate relationships after sexual assault, be gentle with yourself and practice self-compassion. Relationships are challenging for everyone, even without the added layer of sexual assault healing.

EXPERT CONTRIBUTION: CONSENT IN RELATIONSHIPS
Sarah Mathews, MA, LMFT

Ensuring that all parties are consenting to any sexual experience is extremely important and essential to the physical, emotional, psychological, social, sexual, and spiritual well-being of every person. Consent can also be more complex than a one-time "yes" or "no" depending on the nature of the relationship, the kind of sexual encounter you're engaging in, and the needs, abilities, histories, and desires of all parties involved. It can be especially complex for those who have experienced sexual trauma. If you and/or your partner(s) have experienced any kind of sexual boundary violation, move forward with compassion and gentleness toward yourself and each other as you explore, recover, and discover a sense of sexual pleasure and empowerment. The following questions may be helpful to reflect on and talk with your partner(s) about:

1. Do you and your partner(s) understand and recognize their physical, emotional, and cognitive signals of "yes," "no," and "maybe" (and everything in between)?

2. Are you and your partner(s) comfortable choosing and moving forward with their "yes," "no," and "maybe"?

3. Do you and your partner(s) know how and feel comfortable communicating their "yes," "no," and "maybe" to partner(s)?

4. Do you and your partner(s) know what each person needs to create and maintain a safe and respectful environment that uniquely honors each person's levels of consent at any time?

5. Do you and your partner(s) know how to receive and respect someone's "no" to another's "yes" and have a sense of trust and

understanding about how to repair and regain safety in case someone feels unsure, triggered, anxious, or hurt?

It is important to be in an environment and with partners who are respectful and supportive of each person's right to their own level of consent and honor each person's right to change their mind at any time. A "maybe" or "yes" can quickly become a "no" once engaged in an activity, and that is normal and okay! Note that physiological response does not always equal consent. Sometimes our bodies respond to stimuli in a way that does not correspond with what we consent to. Also, if you find yourself in a situation where someone is trying to convince you as a form of "getting consent," let that be a red flag. Healthy sexual experiences are jointly created with all parties participating together. People come to sexual encounters with unique histories, needs, and desires, and it is common for those things to differ.

All of these things (and more) are part of consent. It is common to feel confused, betrayed, or even fearful about any of the above after experiencing sexual trauma, but please note that you do not have to have all the answers, do everything perfectly, or feel completely healed before engaging in a sexual experience or relationship. You are also not alone if in general you're not familiar with or skilled in some or any of the areas mentioned above. It may be helpful to further self-reflect, read additional self-help materials, communicate with your partner(s), and/or seek the support of a mental health professional who can help you explore and sort things through.

Talk about it. Ask questions. Check in with your partner(s). There are "sexy" ways to communicate what might feel good for you and ask your partner(s) about what might feel good to them. Does everyone want to have an overall pleasurable, positive experience? YES! Let's make talking about creating a safe and enjoyable experience a form of foreplay.

LET'S CHECK IN

Healing will come with trying different things, and in order to find what works, you might have to try some things that ultimately don't work. That's okay. What's important is that you're taking steps, one day at a time. Consider the following questions:

- What is something new I can try on my healing journey?
- What are some things I have already tried that I know work?
- What are habits I have that are not helping me on my path to healing?

CHAPTER 12

From Surviving to Thriving

Trauma is destabilizing and can put us into survival mode for an extended period of time. But by being compassionate with ourselves and taking intentional steps to heal, we can transition from surviving to thriving. This chapter offers an opportunity to begin focusing more on the future that you want to create for yourself.

FINDING YOUR WHY

Many survivors find that discovering and pursuing a meaningful purpose is a powerful component of healing and moving forward. Purpose gives us direction and provides the motivation for actions and decisions that we make. It can also help us to reframe stressful situations and facilitate healing from trauma.[66] Here are some examples of survivors' purpose statements.

My purpose is to use art to express my feelings and experiences to empower myself and others.

My purpose is to advocate for change in systems that are not trauma-informed.

My purpose is to educate others about the importance of consent.

My purpose is to create a safe home and safe space for my children to grow and thrive.

My purpose is to rebuild myself, travel, and empower others to pursue happiness.

My purpose is to become a child advocate and help kids start their healing journey early in life.

Finding purpose doesn't mean that you must find purpose *from* your trauma. Although some survivors are drawn to finding meaning in what they experienced, others are not. And that's okay. But taking time to decide what inspires and motivates you will help you to continue to invest in yourself and your future. It can also keep you going on the days when your trauma tries to trick you into believing that there's nothing good ahead for you. By reflecting on your values, interests, and passions, you can determine what matters most to you and use that information to set goals for yourself. No matter how out of reach a goal or dream may seem to be, by taking one step at a time, you can close the distance. One way to begin to find purpose is by supporting other survivors. Sharing your own story can help you to connect with others and realize that you aren't alone. Having a sense of belonging and knowing that there are people who really "get it" can be impactful as you're healing and moving forward. When you share your story with other survivors, it helps you and it also helps them. You can show that healing is possible. Speaking openly about your experiences can also reduce the stigma around sexual assault and empowers others to come forward and seek support themselves.

When I share that I've been assaulted, it opens the door for the person I'm talking with to share their own story, if they so desire. Over the years, many of them have. Making these connections and having moments where we know we're not alone is important. Being a safe person for others to share their experience, validate them, and help them to feel safe is empowering for them and also for us.

EXPERT CONTRIBUTION: THE FUTURE IS BRIGHT

Ammar Charani, author of Purposehood: Transform Your Life, Transform the World

The future is created in the tiny space between expectations and surrender—expectations from infinite desires and unlimited dreams and surrender to the universal force that pulls us toward an existential purpose. If we can create a clear vision of the future and take steps toward increasing its probability, then the possibility of actually bringing that vision into existence is also increased.

Your future and the future of life, humanity, and the universe are bright. There's still so much influence to absorb and exert, so much belonging to offer and accept, so much value to enjoy and create, and so much love to receive and emanate. There is still so much to imagine and desire, so much to learn and gain, so much to create and so much to anticipate and appreciate.

If you're having a hard time finding light in the darkness, keep looking and you *will* eventually find it. For some, that might mean reclaiming aspects of yourself or your life that you thought you'd lost. For others, it might mean finding a reason to endure or seeing a new way forward. Everyone's path is different, but what we all have in common are the strength and clarity we can gain by identifying a purpose that's meaningful to us: our reason for being here—our why.

Everything and everyone that exists has an innate existential purpose to exponentially evolve and expand. But based on our current knowledge, only human beings have the special capabilities of unlimited creativity, infinite desires, and directional choice. We have these unique abilities because we're expo-agents of life—our collective purpose is to help life spread beyond the confines of earth. To fuel our creativity for this monumental mission, we need infinite desires. That's why—like all living organisms—we're selfish, and that's not just okay, it's wonderful. Without the desire to self-preserve, we won't be able to survive, and if we don't survive, we won't have the chance to learn and grow. Selfishness is an ingenious code inserted into every one of our genes to ensure the exponential evolution and expansion of life. That's why we struggle to reach our potential if we're reluctant to embrace our selfishness. But selfishness isn't the only basic genetic code we have.

Altruism is also genetically coded within us to help us expand beyond our self-interests so we can help each other to heal and grow. The altruism coding also encourages us to develop relationships. Without the incentive and ability to give part of ourselves, we won't form relationships with people who can help us to accelerate our evolution and expansion. So, we must be altruistic for selfish reasons; if we don't ensure our self-care and self-growth we won't be able to positively contribute to the world.

If we resist our true nature, we'll lean toward being either primarily altruistic or primarily selfish. But if we embrace our true nature, we'll be altruistic and selfish to varying degrees. With "selfish-altruism" we choose what we want while also being aware that our choices affect others, and even life itself. We might serve many purposes in our lifetime, but our main reason for being alive is our existential purpose or Purposehood.

Identifying our Purposehood means envisioning or subscribing to a positive future and then choosing the role we want to play in creating it. This is the positive role of a creator. Deciding what we want the future to look like and how to invest our time and energy to bring that vision to life is empowering because it's entirely our choice, and learning and growing are part of the process.

Having Purposehood also gives us clarity because it serves as a personal GPS, helping us to make choices that keep us on track so we can accomplish whatever we set out to create or achieve. But in order to be aligned with the nature of the universe and our own nature, our Purposehood must be both selfish and altruistic. Any choice that's against our true nature will cause struggle, which can lead to suffering. The key is to synchronize with the pulling force of the universe's Purposehood to grow and expand exponentially. That will allow us to grow with ease as we're pulled forward by an existential force.

Choose Your Most Empowering Purposehood

Your Purposehood is what you're willing to contribute to the world for what you want to get out of life. And if you're clear enough, the universe—and all its known and unknown forces—will help you get there or show you a better way. This is the power of selfish-altruism, which links what you want with what you're willing to give back for a win-win relationship with existence.

1. Begin with your greatest selfish desire. It's essential to be at ease with your selfish nature so you can guide it toward your ultimate goal.

If you could do or have anything, what would it be?

Your answer must be clear, specific, and selfish.

I want to _____

Examples:

- *I want to be happy.*
- *I want to find community and healing.*
- *I want to live off the grid.*

2. Now, consider what you want to do for the world. If you could do anything, what would it be? Your answer must be clear, specific, and altruistic.

I want to _____

Examples:

- *I want to teach children how to train and care for horses.*
- *I want to share the resources I've learned about with other survivors.*
- *I want to teach young adults about sustainable living practices.*

3. Connect your selfish and altruistic desires with your "why" by writing the word "because" between your selfish and altruistic desires. This causality leads to creation.

I want to _____ (selfish desire) *because*
I want to _____ (altruistic desire).

Examples:

- *I want to be happy because I want to teach children how to train and care for horses.*
- *I want to find community and healing because I want to share the resources I've learned about with other survivors.*
- *I want to live off the grid because I want to teach young adults about sustainable living practices.*

4. Experiment with changing the order to see which statement feels most authentic and inspiring.

I want to _____ (altruistic desire), *because*
I want to _____ (selfish desire).
Examples:

- *I want to teach children how to train and care for horses because I want to be happy.*
- *I want to share the resources I've learned about with other survivors because I want to find community and healing.*
- *I want to teach young adults about sustainable living practices because I want to live off the grid.*

5. Choose your favorite version, keeping in mind that there's no right answer. It's all about you and your feelings. Write down the one you selected, and as you write it, reflect on every word and feel free to change any of them to make your wishes clearer.

_____

6. Write one more version, and instead of linking your wishes with causality (because), link them with *intentionality*. Do this by writing the word "therefore" between the two desires instead of "because."

I will _____, therefore I will
_____.
Examples:

- *I will teach children how to train and care for horses, therefore I will be happy.*
- *I will share the resources I've learned about with other survivors, therefore I will find community and healing.*
- *I will teach young adults about sustainable living practices, therefore I will live off the grid.*

7. Reflect on the intentionality version (#6) and the causality version (#3 and #4) and choose the one that sounds better to you. As always, feel free to change the desires or the words you choose to clearly express them.

8. Write the Purposehood Guiding Star Statement you like best:

_____

_____

Remember, *there's no right or wrong version.* Select the statement that speaks to you in the clearest voice. Your existential purpose is yours to decide, not for anyone else to dictate.

Also, keep in mind that this is just the first draft of your Purposehood Guiding Star Statement—your best guess at the coordinates of your guiding star at this moment. As you pursue this purpose, you'll grow in your awareness, and you can adjust your statement accordingly until it becomes the brightest star in the sky, lighting your way forward every step of the way.

Activate Your Purposehood

Pick one simple thing you can do immediately to activate your Purposehood Guiding Star Statement. It can be as quick and easy as sending a text message or an email. Or it can be an intentional decision to do something that will move you toward your Purposehood or stop doing something that's moving you away from it. Write down this action or decision and make it happen. This is also a productive practice for days when you feel down or unmotivated. Just choose one simple action that will move you closer to your Purposehood and *do it right away.* That small step forward will add resilience, motivation, and a positive mindset to your day.

Since we're human, we sometimes seek what might be bad for us and avoid what might be good, but our Purposehood GPS helps us to make better choices because we can see if they'll move us toward our "why" or away from it. With practice and persistence, we can teach ourselves to only make choices that move us closer to our Purposehood. With this GPS, we're never lost in life. No matter how many delays, detours, or U-turns we take, we'll always be able to find our way forward.

As you think about your Purposehood, it's helpful to keep in mind that Purposehood is in the opposite direction of the choices that make us feel stressed, anxious, or regretful. It's the juncture where happiness, success, and fulfillment meet. If you're receiving these positive signals, then you're on the right road; if not, keep fine-tuning your Purposehood until you *do* receive them.

May you grow with ease.

SUPPORT FROM SURVIVORS: HOW CAN SEXUAL ASSAULT SURVIVORS SUPPORT ONE ANOTHER?

"By giving each other support, sexual assault survivors can create a network of strength and solidarity to help others and help ourselves."

"Share resources!"

"Encourage healthy self-care activities (invite each other for walks or to go to support groups, etc.)."

"Become involved in advocacy efforts in your state."

"Share your story."

"Don't share someone's story without their consent."

"Don't speculate about someone else's trauma."

"Recognize that you don't need to agree or get along with
someone to believe and support them."

"Don't assume they heal the way that you do."

BEING AN ALLY

If you've been assaulted, whether it was recently or in the past, you may feel called to allyship—to be part of a supportive and safe environment for other survivors—but not everyone chooses this path, and that's perfectly okay. You can also be an ally by advocating for better services for survivors and for systemic change in health care, law enforcement, and the courts. If you're sharing your sexual assault healing journey with a loved one, they may find this section helpful. By joining together, we can make change happen.

To be an effective ally and advocate for survivors:

Listen and believe. When a survivor shares their experience with you, listen with empathy and believe what they're telling you. Tell them that you care about them, that you're there for them if they need to talk and that you will support them if they want help accessing resources.

Show active compassion and support. Be understanding and supportive of the survivor's emotions. Ask questions to help understand how to support them and remember that it may be challenging for them to think about how you can help or to ask for help. Consider what you know about them, and take the initiative to do things that will be helpful without being intrusive. That might be bringing them their favorite comfort food, offering to go for a walk, or just sitting with them. Based on what you know about them, do your best to show up for them in a way that they'll appreciate. It can also be helpful to offer practical assistance. For example, would they like someone to drive them to medical appointments? Would they like support researching potential therapists? Do they want someone to go with them to support group sessions?

Educate yourself. Read and research the realities of sexual assault, the myths, the prevalence, and the resources available. Being well informed will help you to better understand and be able to be there for them during their healing process.

Respect boundaries. Remember that the way you choose to process trauma may be very different than how they want to process it. Avoid encouraging them to make decisions or discuss their experience, but be ready to listen when they're ready to share. Since assault can make us feel like we've had control taken away from us, offer them choices. For example, instead of telling them they must report their assault, ask them if they'd like to review resources with you about reporting. Support their decisions and respect their autonomy without judgment.

Support organizations. Advocate for and help organizations that provide resources and support to sexual assault survivors. Offer to volunteer at local shelters, hotlines, or counseling centers. It is also helpful to share information about these resources and encourage other people to get involved.

Speak up against rape culture. Challenge harmful attitudes and beliefs that perpetuate rape culture, including victim blaming, objectification, and normalization of sexual violence. When you hear people make jokes about sexual violence, respectfully educate them. When people around you make victim-blaming remarks, share information about sexual assault myths and redirect the blame to the perpetrator, where it belongs.

Actively intervene. There are many ways to help keep each other safe. Offer to give a ride home to a friend who is vulnerable due to intoxication or check in with one another to make sure everyone feels safe. If you witness a situation that could lead to sexual assault, find a safe way to help and intervene. You can create a distraction to de-escalate a situation, without leaving the aggressor and the individual alone. If you can, ask the individual who appears to be at risk if they need help. You can also say, "Would you like me to stay with you?" or offer to leave with them and go to a different location. Make sure that the aggressor is not listening, as this could lead to escalation.

Do not hesitate to ask other people to support you in intervening if you think they would be more effective—if, for example, the aggressor is their friend and can help remove them from the situation. You can also ask an authority figure like a bartender or bouncer to intervene, or call law enforcement. Make the choices that are safe for you and the person who needs help. Afterward, check in with the person who was at risk, offer them support, and tell them how to access resources. Our actions matter, and we can play a part in protecting others.

Take care of yourself. Being an ally can lead to burnout and secondary trauma. You can best support others only when you are caring for yourself, too. So be sure you're keeping up your own self-care, including eating healthy and balanced meals, getting enough sleep every night, being mindful of your stress levels, spending time outside, and exercising regularly. Use relaxation techniques that work for you, and take your vacation days. Be mindful of your own limitations and triggers.

VICARIOUS AND SECONDARY TRAUMA

For our loved ones and support network to best support us on our healing journey, it is helpful for them to know that secondary and vicarious trauma can impact them. By being aware of this, and having their own mental health plan and support, they will be in a better position to offer us support.

Vicarious trauma is when professionals experience a shift in their attitude or worldview after prolonged exposure to hearing and treating people who have experienced trauma and suffering. This shift can affect their sense of safety, ability to trust others, intimacy, and sense of control.

Secondary trauma is when someone is significantly affected by hearing a story about a traumatic experience that someone else experienced. This can happen to those in helping professions (law enforcement, therapists, and social workers), as well as the loved ones of trauma survivors. The symptoms of secondary trauma can look very similar to PTSD symptoms.

Supporting someone who has experienced assault takes strength and resilience, so encourage the people in your support network to stay healthy, take time for self-care activities, and to rely on their own social support networks. Urge them to give themselves the same level of compassion that they're giving you, and tell them that therapy can help to reduce and alleviate the symptoms of secondary trauma.

RECLAIMING WHO YOU WERE AND CHOOSING WHO YOU WILL BE

The sexual assault isn't our identity, it's not a life sentence, and it doesn't have to stop us from living the lives we want. Yes, the trauma of sexual assault is life-changing and it takes time and effort to heal, but the future is still bright for us.

For many survivors, the healing journey can be confusing. It's not linear, and zigzags can feel like setbacks instead of progress. Sometimes it seems as if the hardest thing we have to do is grieve and move on from the pieces of ourselves that we feel we've lost. Some survivors say they feel as if they lost their innocence, their optimism, and their positive memories. The pain can consume us and it can consume our future unless we address it and find freedom from it.

Parts of you might feel very much the same as they did before the assault as you work on healing. Other parts of you might feel new and different and take time to get used to. For example, while working on your healing, you may rediscover a love for fitness and health that you felt you had lost. But through healing and working on triggers, you feel safe enough to go running again and rebuild that part of your life. On the other hand, you might realize that by healing through the trauma, you've discovered a piece of you that is passionate about the arts as a way to express yourself. Perhaps now you love to dance as a way of releasing tension in your body. Or you realize you have a knack for leading peer support groups. I highly encourage you to safely try as much as you can while slowly pushing yourself out of your comfort zone. I guarantee you will learn more about yourself in the process.

Values

Another way to get to know yourself again is to think about your values and commit to making decisions that are in alignment with those values. Becoming aware of our values helps us to know ourselves better, because our values guide our choices, actions, and what we prioritize. Thinking about what you value might sound overwhelming or abstract, but here are some questions to help you to identify them:

- What inspires you?
- What are you unwilling to compromise on?
- What is important to you?

I can share some of my own answers to help show how this helps. I get inspired when I'm thinking about or working on survivors resources that didn't exist when I needed them. I am unwilling to compromise my health and my personal growth. It is important to me to have horses in my life and be able to step out onto a porch and feel close to nature. Based on this, I value helping survivors, personal growth, health, and being outside daily. So, if I'm presented with a choice that goes against these values, I can say no with more confidence.

Goals

While dealing with mental health challenges, it can feel like you don't have direction, which can make anxiety, depression, and confusion worse. Having objective goals and breaking them down into manageable steps can make moving forward feel less daunting, and reaching each milestone can increase your self-esteem and motivation.

1. Define your goals. Being specific is important, and making them SMART (specific, measurable, achievable, relevant, time-bound) goals can be helpful. For example, *By December of next year I will SCUBA dive in Cozumel, Mexico.*
2. Break the goal down into individual steps. In our example, some steps include:

a. Find a therapist to work on building confidence and identifying triggers.

b. Find a diving school.

c. Become a certified SCUBA diver.

d. Get a passport.

e. Calculate the cost.

f. Save money for the trip.

g. Plan the trip (lodging and diving team).

h. Request the time off from work.

3. Prioritize the steps and put timelines on each item:

a. Find a therapist to work on building confidence and identifying triggers.—Complete by January 1.

b. Find a diving school.—Complete by January 1.

c. Become a certified SCUBA diver.—Be certified by March 1.

d. Get a passport. A passport takes up to 180 days from the
application, so I need to start this process by June 1 to be on
the safe side.

4. Plan regular check-ins, and be flexible as needed. For example,
during COVID-19 people had to push many trips and activities
out as a result of the shutdown. If that happens, set aside time to
review your goals and identify which goals you can still work
on in the meantime, and move the date for your large goal back.
Don't give up!

5. Celebrate each milestone. Do this in whatever ways motivate
and work best for you. Personally, I love a visual checklist posted
in my office so I can physically check each item off. Some people
like to use apps to keep track of things. Experiment and find out
what works well for you.

Dreaming of and Creating Your Future

People will say that after they purchase a blue car, they start to see them everywhere. We notice things more when our mind is programmed to look for them. We can use this idea to actively create and picture our future. People have done this in different ways, such as by using vision boards (vision board nights are a great activity to do with new and developing friendships), Pinterest boards, or writing out their dreams and vision.

One exercise a dear friend suggested was to write down in first person and present tense how I wanted my life to look in five years and read it every morning before I got out of bed. At first, I had doubts about this idea, but I found over time that it worked. By telling myself, "I am a financially independent woman working as a nurse," I started to think that way when making decisions. When presented with options and opportunities, I would make decisions by asking myself, "What decision would help me on my journey to become a nurse?" or "Is this something that a financially independent person would do?" And slowly, over time, I saw myself living a life more in alignment with my dreams.

Building Routines

Trauma shakes the world as we know it and makes us feel like we have less structure, safety, and control over ourselves and our environment. Building routines can help to increase our lives' structure and predictability, which relieves anxiety and stress. These routines also can help us build healthy habits, which increase our resilience.

Begin with small and manageable steps. Look at your life and current routines and consider what area would benefit the most from adding more structure. For example, would adding a healthy bedtime routine be beneficial? Or do you feel that a structured morning routine is more needed? Be patient with yourself, because creating new habits takes time.

Getting Through the Hard Days

Over time and with a lot of healing work, the hard days will become fewer. But there will still be some, and sometimes they will sneak up on you. Bad days do not mean you have gone backward in your healing. Being able to recognize that you're having a hard day, identifying the trigger, and knowing what tools might help you get through the hard day are all wins. Give yourself permission to take a break, breathe, and make yourself your top priority. On some days that might mean taking care of your basic needs (showering and making yourself eat). You might need to utilize a hotline to access resources in your area (see page 36). Reach out to people you trust who support you (see page 87). Push yourself to do something that brings you joy; consider your glimmers and seek them out (see page 221). Focus on the fact that you have survived your assault and your healing journey this far, and trust that you can get through today as well.

I want to assure you that this healing journey is worth taking. Always remember that you are not responsible for your assault. You didn't choose your trauma response, how your loved ones reacted to your disclosure, or how institutions such as the legal system or health care system supported you in the reporting and court process. You have a very important choice to make—the choice of how your life will look moving forward. There will be obstacles and times when your trauma rears its ugly head, but you can always choose to heal—for yourself and for the survivors who will join you.

SUPPORT FROM SURVIVORS:
WHAT'S IN STORE FOR YOU NOW?

"I've come to learn what to expect in a healthy relationship. Especially when it comes to sex. My body, my rules. Drunk, sober, or otherwise."

"I have a sweet little boy, a kind husband, a beautiful home and pets. I'm hundreds of miles from my abuser, so I don't have to see him often. I feel safe where I live now, although I still often see men as dangerous or untrustworthy. Someday I will confront him, but I'm just not there yet. For now, I am just trying to enjoy my life and be an attentive, strong mother for my son. I never want him or any of my future children to have to experience what I went through, and I hope with all my heart that I can give them the tools they need to fight back if it does happen."

"Right now, I am just a sophomore in high school. I have big, big plans to go into the medical field, and I want to either be a nurse practitioner or a physician. Right now, I also have a good support net of people to fall back on when I need them. My family is closer than ever, and soon I will be going to college and moving out and starting my own family hopefully."

"Trying to move forward, I recognize that I am a strong person and I want to try and use my experiences to help lift up other people."

"I'm in grad school and applying to law school."

"I'm going to continue with my social group to drive reform and campaign for change, and I'm also starting my own personal journey into college to do psychology and counseling, as I want to help others."

"I have now met a supportive partner and I want to go on and have a family. I'd like to start a blog about my recovery and all that happened so that I can support others and hopefully help someone else who felt as lonely as I did."

"I plan to advocate my ass off and be an obnoxiously persistent voice that holds institutions accountable for their failures. Survivors deserve better."

"I will have eternal peace and joy whether he goes to jail or not. I will move forward."

"I like singing. I like writing. I have fresh new friends. I have a sense of belonging in feminism and the LGBTQ+ community. I'm learning to love my body step by step. I don't know what I'm going to do with all of that, but that's me right now, and there's potential here. So we'll see what the future holds."

Sidney's Story

I remember feeling powerless and not in control of my body for a long time after being sexually assaulted. I found myself second-guessing my decisions and my motivations for things. I felt like I had lost my sense of self and what brought me joy.

But I also remember—even more clearly than my assault—the first solo trip I took. I remember one day waking up in a fog and feeling like if I didn't book a plane ticket that day, I was never going to go anywhere. And so I did. And I remember feeling scared shitless but also more powerful than I had ever felt. I had made the decision, not only to face my fear of flying, but to face my fear of not living. I remember sweating on the plane and checking the flight tracker every ten minutes hoping by some miracle I was already at my destination. I remember the older woman next to me striking up a kind conversation and telling me how brave she thought I was for going on a trip alone and not waiting to live my life. I had never thought of it as brave. I just thought if I didn't do it, maybe I'd never do anything.

When I arrived in Paris, I was jet-lagged and in a state of culture shock. But that all faded, and soon I felt resourceful, confident in my decisions, and absolutely joyous. I walked around that city like we were good friends. Paris was kind to me and brought out parts of myself that I forgot were there. I trusted and followed my instincts. I laughed with so many people. I flirted and felt good about it. I ate some of the most delicious food and found so much power in the fact that this trip was mine. That my experience was my own. That I was in control. That the joy I was seeking was here.

Since then, I have taken nine solo trips across five continents. I have learned so much about myself and the world around me. I realize how big this world is. How much possibility fills it and how much joy there is in it. I have met so many people from so many different walks of life with so many different perspectives. I've had my mind changed. I've grown. I've cried. I've laughed. I've danced. I come back each time renewed and challenged, feeling ready to take on the world around me.

Solo travel for me means stepping out of my comfort zone for the sake of growth and happiness. It means striking up a conversation with someone you may not normally talk to. Or laughing with someone over Google Translate. It means learning a new dance from someone else's culture. Trying new foods. Changing my path. Being okay with sitting in silence and loneliness. Saying yes, saying no, and being confident in either answer. I am a better woman because I travel. I am kinder. Softer. Fiercer. I speak my mind more. I'm resourceful and determined. I'm more aware of the beauty in the world and in myself. I know who I am. I have reclaimed my sense of self.

One of the biggest gifts solo travel has given me, that I lost after my assault, is being self-aware. I feel like I am better able to identify emotions in my body and name them and feel less intimidated by them. I feel in control of how I react to my environment, and I can understand the root of those reactions better. I'm not scared to feel. Even sadness doesn't feel like it will turn into a downward spiral anymore. My sense of self has returned, and with it, peace within my entire body even when chaos is happening around me.

My journey has not been an easy one. Getting on a plane didn't fix everything. I've had to do the difficult work in between the flights. I've had to come to terms with the impact my assault had on me and learn to navigate the journey to joy. And the journey isn't linear. And there's no finish line to cross. Joy comes in moments. Like graduating from school even though you doubted you would ever finish. Or realizing you're the first one on the dance floor, when years ago, you would have never stepped foot into a club. Asking someone on a date even though you're nervous. A milestone birthday. Telling someone you love them. Joy comes to me when I recognize the progress I've made. When I can hold both my happiness and my sadness. The journey is forever, and I'm so proud of the work I've done so far.

If I could tell survivors anything, it would be to find the thing that brings you joy and don't let anyone take it from you. In all my adventures, I've had so many people—even the people closest to me—try to discourage me from traveling by myself. It's hard when people don't understand your dream or your joy. But don't let that deter you. You know you best. Reclaim your happiness. Only you can decide what that is.

Love,

Sidney

LET'S CHECK IN

We fight against sexual assault and rape culture by using our voices, supporting one another, and flourishing in our lives despite the trauma we faced. Our trauma didn't make us strong; we did. Your strength and resilience brought you to where you are today. As you reflect on your journey, consider the following:

- What brings you joy?
- What values do you choose to incorporate into your life?
- What is one dream that you have, and what is one small step you can take today to walk toward that dream?

You deserve to live a big and beautiful life. What that looks like will be different for everyone, and that's part of what makes this community so resourceful and creative. I hope that you feel the excitement that comes with getting to know yourself again and seeing the doors that are open for you.

A Note from the Author

After I was assaulted, I felt lost and unsure of how to move forward. And I felt that way again after reporting the crime to law enforcement, and again after the trial for my case concluded. This book was born out of that feeling of being lost, and out of my deep desire to help other survivors find their way. My hope is that the information and resources in this book have helped you to believe that your voice, resilience, and strength are stronger than your trauma. And I hope it helped you to believe that our futures are worth striving for.

Empowering yourself with information is a huge step. The information included in this book is meant to be a foundation. Continue to seek out knowledge and understanding, and keep checking in with yourself and your needs. Be intentional about your healing, including making changes in your healing plan as you move forward. Engage in conversation with supporters and survivors, and advocate for yourself and for other survivors. We are the evidence and we can advocate for change, support other survivors, and educate others. Together, we can make the world a better, safer place.

More Support from the Experts

In this section, you'll find additional advice from expert contributors.

EXPERT CONTRIBUTION:
MILITARY SEXUAL TRAUMA (MST)
REPORTING
Bree Theising-Stair, Sexual Violence Advocate

Military sexual trauma (MST) is defined as anyone who has experienced sexual violence or sexual harassment during their time in the military. A military member has the right to the military process and the civilian process of reporting, exam, and support.

Sexual Assault Response Coordinator (SARC): These are represented in each branch of the military. They oversee sexual violence policies and protocols within their branch of the military.

Sexual Assault Prevention and Response Coordinator (SAPR): These are represented in each branch of the military. They are the sexual violence advocates for military personnel. They can support victims/survivors during the reporting process. They have to also have had the state mandated forty-plus–hour training.

Sexual Assault Forensic Exam (SAFE): A forensic evidence collection exam completed by a military-trained medical professional.

The medical professional completing the exam has done extra training specifically for completing evidence collection.

Unrestricted: This is an option for reporting for victims/survivors who would like to proceed with an official investigation, command notification, medical services, and victim advocacy.

Restricted: This is an option for reporting for victims/survivors who would *not* like to proceed with an official investigation or command notification but would like to receive medical services and victim advocacy.

Military Protective Order (MPO): Issued by the unit commanders at the request of the victim/survivor or SAPR. These orders are delivered verbally and/or in writing at no cost to the victim/survivor. These orders can be granted for ten days or more. These orders can only be enforced on active duty military bases/posts, etc. Both the victim/survivor and perpetrator must be on active duty for this order to be in place. This also can only be enforced in the commanding officer's area of supervision (i.e., unit or base of command).

Sexual Harassment: Within seventy-two hours (three days) of receiving a complaint of sexual harassment, the commanding officer who took the complaint must forward all information to their next in command and the independent investigative team. The goal of that investigative team is to have their investigation completed in fourteen days.

EXPERT CONTRIBUTION: THE POWER OF HORSES IN HEALING

Sydney Condrashoff, Equus Coach, Master Facilitator, Horse Trainer

Horses have been healing and supporting us humans for hundreds of years, and I truly believe that their gifts in supporting healing come from a commonality that they share with us. Horses pave the way for what it looks like to connect and share from a place of authenticity, congruency, and duality. They offer us a beautiful space to honor our experience while also holding space for another in theirs. Their main goal in life is safety, and they understand that their safety comes from numbers, aka the herd. We are wired very similarly to horses. We need connection and community in order to survive and feel safe, yet we have built a society where isolation, individualism, and doing it yourself is celebrated and sought after.

Horses operate the majority of the time in a parasympathetic nervous function, also known as *rest and digest*. They are energy preservers and typically spend their day connected to presence, stillness, and one another. It enables them to be fit to respond if a threat were to approach. At birth, humans are wired very similarly, but as we begin to learn language and make meaning of things, we begin to spend the majority of time in sympathetic nervous function, also known as *fight or flight*. I believe this comes from an underlying desire to feel accepted by others and experience a sense of belonging. We run around stressed on the to-do lists and the worries of what tomorrow will bring, and that keeps us separated from connection, community, and, most of all, ourselves.

When we connect with horses, we get to experience what it's like to be completely in the moment. We're being present with ourselves, with the horse, and with the remarkable biofeedback loop that happens when we explore connection with an animal that's hard-wired to read whether we're being honest and congruent with who we are, an animal that is paying attention to what we are energetically putting out there and what we're saying with our body language. If we express a personality or identity that isn't aligned with who we truly are, horses have an incredible gift for pointing that out. They don't care about who you say you are, how much money you make, or what happened in your past. They care about you being present in your body, connected to your emotional state, and honest with what you're feeling, whatever that may be. Being connected to yourself increases safety in the herd because others can understand what you need, who you are, and how you support the herd. It is a nonjudgmental, loving, and welcoming space where you discover that being raw and truthful *is* the path to connection and intimacy. It always has been.

When you experience this type of connection, you know it's possible, and that gives you a reference for other relationships and builds a bridge to everything around you. The herd offers us a safer path forward with nature as our road map and our hearts as our guide.

Contributor Biographies

Experts

Amanda Schonhardt has been a child protection social worker in Minnesota for fifteen years. She enjoys working with families and meeting them where they are at.

After studying with Sufi masters for a decade, **Ammar Charani** earned his engineering degree and then turned to entrepreneurship, founding more than thirty businesses. A University of Central Florida and Harvard alum, he's the founder of YPO Change Makers and Purposehood®, focusing on existential purpose. His books and life engineering course are highly acclaimed by CEOs. purposehood.org/

Angela Goens, registered dietitian, has spent her entire career working in the mental health field, specifically serving clients who deal with eating disorders, chemical dependency, depression, anxiety, and trauma. She is the owner of Rooted Nutrition Services, which is focused on supporting those with marginalized identities who struggle with eating disorders and disordered eating patterns. She is also the co-creator of the first ever Black Indigenous People of Color (BIPOC) Eating Disorders Conference, which is focused on improving ways to better meet the needs of those often overlooked by traditional treatment and highlight amazing expert BIPOC presenters.

Brandan Borgos, an attorney and legal analyst in Minneapolis, has advised clients in family law, criminal defense, landlord-tenant law, and cannabis policy since 2010. When he's not practicing law, he can be found doing martial arts, yoga, meditating, or with his nose buried in a fantasy novel.

Bree Theising-Stair is an advocate with over a decade of experience working alongside victims/survivors and professionals eradicating sexual violence and promoting healing. Bree specializes in medical advocacy, sexual assault kits, and has done direct services. She continues to fight for those who may be silenced.

Cate Schultz is the owner/operator of ELC Fitness 24/7 in Morris, Minnesota. With a background in psychology/human services and therapeutic coaching, she loves providing a space for others to experience community and fitness together. With her husband, she owns multiple businesses, and they are passionate about positively impacting the lives of others through their work.

Dr. Heather J. Peters is a full professor of psychology at the University of Minnesota, Morris, and a licensed psychologist. Dr. Peters's publications focus on the development of culturally sensitive interventions and programs that improve the health and well-being of people who experience marginalization. Dr. Peters partners with organizations to create just and equitable environments. A few of Dr. Peters's awards include the Cesar E. Chavez Award, Horace T. Morse–University of Minnesota Award for Outstanding Contributions to Undergraduate Education, and the Charlotte Striebel Equity Award.

Justin Boardman, former detective, spent fifteen years in law enforcement, with the West Valley City Police Department, Utah. Justin co-authored a Trauma-Informed Victim Interview for adult victims of trauma. Justin now trains internationally on a variety of subjects including domestic and sexual violence investigations, trauma response, and multidisciplinary teams.

Kathryn Marsh is a career special victim's prosecutor of twenty years. She currently serves as a Special Victim's Litigation Expert for the US Army's Office of Special Trial Counsel. Ms. Marsh is a professional trainer for prosecutors, staff, law enforcement, educational institutions, and community organizations and is an adjunct professor with Fox Valley, National Criminal Justice Training Center. Additionally, Ms. Marsh has assisted in drafting legislation and has testified before the Maryland legislature on special victims' legislation for several years.

Lalania Walker is an enrolled member of the Muscogee Creek Nation and descendant of the White Earth Nation and Mississippi Band of Choctaw Indians. She is the White Earth Tribal Child Advocacy Center Coordinator who oversees the program operations, forensic interviews, family advocacy, and SANE-P evaluations. She has advanced training in forensic interviewing of children, and currently conducts forensic interviews for law enforcement and child protection agencies within and surrounding the White Earth Reservation boundaries. Her career focuses on investigations of child abuse, child safety, and ensuring that families have what they need on their healing journey.

Lauren Weingarten (she/her) is a credentialed victim advocate (NACP) and certified trauma support specialist. She is the voice and founder of MTMV Community Support Network, one of the first social media–based support communities established for survivors and supporters of survivors. Before MTMV, Ms. Weingarten had a successful, decades-long career working behind the scenes in TV and film production. Her best friend is a pup named Tofu and she loves pizza, falafel, and tending to her plants.

Lindsay Nelson's calling has always been women's health. She graduated from nursing school in 2008 and went right into labor and delivery. She worked as a labor and delivery and NICU nurse for ten years and then completed a graduate nurse-midwifery program. Since then, she has provided full-scope midwifery care in a metropolitan area. Her special interest areas include maternal mental health, care of families experiencing fetal loss, and promotion and participation in an autonomous health care model in which people have the right of choice.

Maggie Wagner is communications coordinator at the Legal Action Center in New York. She has a master's degree in human rights studies from Columbia University, where she completed the thesis "Black Women's Security and Barriers to Reporting Sexual Assault to Police: 'It Couldn't Be Any Worse of a System.'"

Melissa Hoppmeyer is a former special victims prosecutor with over a decade of experience advocating for survivors. She currently serves as a policy adviser on gender-based violence for the military. Ms. Hoppmeyer has assisted in developing and implementing policy and laws to help ensure that gender-based violence survivors are treated fairly throughout the judicial system.

Patricia Bathory, MBA, MACP, CCC, is a psychotherapist and the founder and general manager of an import/export business. She is a relationship expert, speaker, and author of *Connected: Building Relationships to Achieve Success and Make a Lasting Impact*.

Dr. Ruth Goins is an emergency veterinarian in Chicago, Illinois. She received her DVM from the University of California, Davis.

When she's not at the hospital, she likes to spend time with her two cats, cooking, working out, and exploring the city.

Ryan J. Krupp is an attorney in St. Louis, Missouri. He has prosecuted many perpetrators of sexual assault both criminally and civilly, currently focusing on helping survivors in their battle against some of the world's biggest companies, including insurance companies, hotels, medical providers, retail stores, and many others.

Sarah Mathews is a licensed marriage and family therapist and supervisor who specializes in highly sensitive individuals, relationships, and sexuality. She graduated from the University of Minnesota with a BIS (bachelor of individual studies) degree in psychology, relationship studies, and communication, and obtained a master's degree in counseling psychology from the Institute of Transpersonal Psychology in Palo Alto, California. You may find her frolicking in nature or happily lost in one of her creative pursuits.

Shelly Fisher is a detective in the City of Waukesha Police Department. She is a thirty-year veteran who has worked the last sixteen years as a sensitive crimes detective. Her focus is crimes against children, the elderly, and victims of domestic abuse. She specializes in forensic interviews and child death investigations. She shares, "It's been an honor to serve the most vulnerable victims throughout my career."

Sydney Condrashoff is an Equus Coach, life coach, master facilitator, horse trainer, and intuitive horse listener. She is passionate about helping others heal from their pasts, get clear on where they're headed, and find the courage to move forward in their lives.

Survivor Stories

Celeste Mergens is a specialist in bridging difficult cultural divides and overcoming trauma. She is the founder of Days for Girls, a global award-winning organization that has reached 3 million women and girls in 145 countries. She's filled three passports with global evidence that what connects us is far more than what divides us. Her book *The Power of Days: A Story of Resilience, Dignity, and the Fight for Women's Equity* shares proof that we can all make a difference. She has been featured in Oprah's O magazine and *Forbes* and has been named Conscious Company Global Impact Entrepreneur Top Ten Women, and Women's Economic Forum's Woman of the Decade, to name a few.

Isabella Grosso is a California native who dedicates her time and energy to her one true passion in life: educating and teaching the power of dance to survivors of sexual abuse and sex trafficking. Isabella shares a similar story: She was first abused at the young age of five. By the time she was twelve, seven different people had abused her, and unfortunately not one of those people was a stranger to her. Years of attempting to heal from trauma led her back to her first love of dance. Dance is still the one place where she can always rediscover her power and reconnect to her body. In this way, it's been her safekeeper ever since.

Dr. Michelle Davenport, DNP-RN, was born and raised in New York City, is married, a mother of four children, with seventeen grandchildren and two great-grandchildren. Michelle is a faith community nurse, attends House of Praise COGIC in Saint Paul, and is an Ambassador Spokeswoman for the American Heart Association Go Red for Women.

Sidney holds a bachelor of finance degree from the University of Minnesota and is on the leadership board for the Visibility Impact Fund. She is passionate about travel, never passes up a chance to go dancing, and believes in creating as much joy as possible in her life.

Steven is from Baltimore, Maryland, where he is currently in nursing school and plans to pursue cardiology after graduation. His hobbies include staying active by going to the gym or for long walks and hanging out with friends, family, and his dog, Leo. His favorite season is fall and his favorite movie is *Mamma Mia!* He is also fluent in Greek.

Acknowledgments

On this journey I have had the opportunity to meet incredible people, and this book has a team behind it that showed immense dedication to helping to make it happen. It has been humbling and beautiful to watch this book gain so much support. Thank you to everyone who believed in this book. Thank you to everyone who believed in me.

To my family: Mom, thank you for showing me what it is to be strong and loving. You have always done everything possible to make sure that I could make this book come to life. Sheridan, you may be my little sister, but I have always looked up to you. You have made sure that I was never alone in this endeavor. NJ, your unwavering support has been a source of inspiration for me throughout this journey. To Jennifer and Travis, thank you for believing and supporting me. And to my beloved dad, your unwavering love and wisdom have continued to guide me even in your absence. You have shown me what bravery looks like when going against the wind.

To my friends: Thank you to everyone who touched my life as I was writing this book. In every stage of this journey, you offered encouragement and support. I appreciate all of you.

To the experts and advocates: Thank you for believing in my mission to fill a gap in the world of sexual assault advocacy, being so generous with your time and expertise, and for being committed to helping survivors of sexual assault.

To my agent, Claire Gerus, thank you for believing in the importance of this book and finding the right home for it.

To my editors, Nana K. Twumasi and Natalie Bautista, thank you for helping to shape the book into the best resource it can possibly be. I am incredibly fortunate for your support.

To my book architect and writing coach, Toni Robino, this book exists because of you and your unwavering support and encouragement. You have been part of this process every step of the way, and your dedication to building a better world with books helped to bring this book to life. Just as I hope this book can be a guiding light for many, you have been that guiding light for me.

To all survivors of sexual violence: This book would not have been possible without the survivors who inspire me with your strength, trust, and resilience. Your voices are the heart of this book. As we move forward, may this book serve as a testament to our collective dedication to making the world a better place one step at a time.

Notes

1. "Sexual Assault," Office on Violence Against Women, Department of Justice, September 3, 2020, https://www.justice.gov/ovw/sexual-assault

2. "Rape," FBI, n.d., https://ucr.fbi.gov/crime-in-the-u.s./2013/crime-in-the-u.s.-2013/violent-crime/rape

3. "An Updated Definition of Rape," Office of Public Affairs, September 16, 2014, https://www.justice.gov/opa/pr/attorney-general-eric-holder-announces-revisions-uniform-crime-report-s-definition-rape#:~:text=T%20he%20longstanding%2C%20C%20

4. Ibid.

5. "What Is Sexual Consent? | Facts about Rape & Sexual Assault," https://www.plannedparenthood.org/learn/relationships/sexual-consent

6. Department of Justice, Office of Justice Programs, Bureau of Justice Statistics, National Crime Victimization Survey, 2010–2016 (2017).

7. Snyder, Howard. "Sexual Assault of Young Children as Reported to Law Enforcement: Victim, Incident, and Offender Characteristics. A NIBRS Statistical Report," https://eric.ed.gov/?id=ED446834

8. Planty et al., "Female Victims of Sexual Violence, 1994–2010," https://bjs.ojp.gov/content/pub/pdf/fvsv9410.pdf

9. Department of Justice, Office of Justice Programs, Bureau of Justice Statistics, National Crime Victimization Survey, 2010–2014 (2015).

10. Yuan et al., "Risk Factors for Physical Assault and Rape among Six Native American Tribes," https://doi.org/10.1177/0886260506294239

11. Linklater, Renee. *Decolonizing Trauma Work: Indigenous Stories and Strategies*. Fernwood Publishing, 2020.

12. Deer, Sarah. *The Beginning and End of Rape: Confronting Sexual Violence in Native America*. University of Minnesota Press, 2015.

13. Broman-Fulks, J. J., Ruggiero, K. J., Hanson, R. F., Smith, D. W., Resnick, H. S., Kilpatrick, D. G., & Saunders, B. E. (2007). "Sexual assault disclosure in relation to adolescent mental health: Results from the National Survey of Adolescents." *Journal of Clinical Child and Adolescent Psychology*, 36, 260–266.

14. Smith, D. W., Letourneau, E. J., Saunders, B. E., Kilpatrick, D. G., Resnick, H. S., & Best, C. L. (2000). "Delay in disclosure of childhood rape: Results from a national survey." *Child Abuse & Neglect*, 24, 273–287.

15. Bracha, "Freeze, Flight, Fight, Fright, Faint: Adaptationist Perspectives on the Acute Stress Response Spectrum." *CNS spectrums* vol. 9, 9 (2004): 679–85 doi: 10.1017 /s1092852900001954

16. Ibid.

17. Kallivayalil et al., "The Coping Skills and Quality of Life among Rape Survivors: A Descriptive Study from Kerala." *Indian J Psychiatry* vol. 64(4) (2022): 387–394 doi: 10.4103/indianjpsychiatry.indianjpsychiatry_78_22

18. Rich, G, "Massage Therapy for PTSD, Trauma, and Anxiety." *RUDN Journal of Psychology and Pedagogics* 3 (2013): 60–66. WEB. doi: 10.22363/2313-1683-2013-3-60-66

19. Ding et al., "Efficacy and Safety of Acupuncture in Treating Post-Traumatic Stress Disorder." *Medicine* vol. 99, 26 (2020): e20700

20. Postma et al., "Pelvic Floor Muscle Problems Mediate Sexual Problems in Young Adult Rape Victims." *The Journal of Sexual Medicine* vol. 10, 8 (2013): 1978–1987 doi:10.1111/jsm.12196

21. L. Tice et al., "Sexual Abuse in Patients with Eating Disorders." *Psychiatric Medicine* 7, no. 4 (December 31, 1988): 257–267.

22. "Crime Victims' Rights Act," July 22, 2016, https://www.justice.gov/usao /resources/crime-victims-rights-ombudsman/victims-rights-act

23. Lonsway, Kimberly, Joanne Archambault, and David Lasik. "False Reports: Moving beyond the Issue to Successfully Investigate and Prosecute Non-Stranger Sexual Assault." National Sexual Violence Resource Center, 2009. https://www .nsvrc.org/publications/articles/false-reports-moving-beyond-issue-successfully -investigate-and-prosecute-non-s

24. Rennison. "Rape and Sexual Assault: Reporting to Police and Medical Attention, 1992–2000," https://bjs.ojp.gov/content/pub/pdf/rsarp00.pdf

25. Know Your Title IX (2021). "The Cost of Reporting: Perpetrator Retaliation, Institutional Betrayal, and Student Survivor Pushout." Retrieved from https://www.knowy ourix.org/wp-content/uploads/2021/03/Know-Your-IX-2021-Report-Final-Copy.pdf

26. Marshall, Tony F. *Restorative Justice: An Overview*. London: Home Office, 1999.

27. "Rights of Victims," March 22, 2022, https://www.justice.gov/enrd/rights-victims #:~:text=The%20right%20to%20proceedings%20free,the%20victim's%20 dignity%20and%20privacy

28. "The Criminal Justice System: Statistics | RAINN," https://www.rainn.org/statistics /criminal-justice-system

29. Ibid.

30. *Berger v. United States*, 295 U.S. 78, 88 (1935).

31. Fourth Edition (2017) of the *Criminal Justice Standards for the Prosecution Function*.

32. "Beyond a Reasonable Doubt," n.d. LII / Legal Information Institute, https://www .law.cornell.edu/wex/beyond_a_reasonable_doubt

33. Lonsway, Kimberly, Joanne Archambault, and David Lasik. "False Reports: Moving beyond the Issue to Successfully Investigate and Prosecute Non-Stranger Sexual Assault." National Sexual Violence Resource Center, 2009. https://www.nsvrc.org /publications/articles/false-reports-moving-beyond-issue-successfully-investigate -and-prosecute-non-s

34. Perpetrators of Sexual Violence: Statistics | RAINN, https://www.rainn.org /statistics/perpetrators-sexual-violence

35. National Center for State Courts (2019). "Criminal Caseloads—Types of Cases Filed." Retrieved from: https://www.ncsc.org/~/media/Files/PDF/Topics/Court %20Management/Caseload/Criminal_Caseload_Types_of_Cases_Filed.ashx

36. Bureau of Justice Statistics (2018). State Court Processing Statistics. Retrieved from: https://www.bjs.gov/content/pub/pdf/scps18.pdf

37. National Center for State Courts (2019). "Criminal Caseloads—Types of Cases Filed." Retrieved from: https://www.ncsc.org/~/media/Files/PDF/Topics/Court %20Management/Caseload/Criminal_Caseload_Types_of_Cases_Filed.ashx

38. Bureau of Justice Statistics (2018). State Court Processing Statistics. Retrieved from: https://www.bjs.gov/content/pub/pdf/scps18.pdf

39. "Beyond a Reasonable Doubt."

40. Kessler et al., "Prevalence, Severity, and Comorbidity of 12-Month DSM-IV Disorders in the National Comorbidity Survey Replication."

41. Pratt, Brody, and Gu. "Antidepressant Use in Persons Aged 12 and Over: United States, 2005–2008." *NCHS Data Brief* (2011): 76, 1–8. https://pubmed.ncbi.nlm.nih .gov/22617183/.

42. Sarah E. Ullman et al., "Trauma Histories, Substance Use Coping, PTSD, and Problem Substance Use among Sexual Assault Victims." *Addictive Behaviors* 38, no. 6 (June 1, 2013): 2219–2223, https://doi.org/10.1016/j.addbeh.2013.01.027

43. Ami Laws and Jacqueline M. Golding. "Sexual Assault History and Eating Disorder Symptoms among White, Hispanic, and African-American Women and Men." *American Journal of Public Health* 86, no. 4 (April 1, 1996): 579–582, https://doi.org/10.2105/ajph.86.4.579

44. Kyle T. Ganson et al., "Sexual Assault Victimization and Eating Disorders among College-Enrolled Men." *Journal of Interpersonal Violence* 37, no. 7–8 (September 20, 2020): NP5143–66, https://doi.org/10.1177/0886260520958634

45. National Institute of Mental Health, 2009. "Anxiety Disorders." Retrieved from https://www.nimh.nih.giv/heath/publications/anxiety-disorders/nimhanxiety.pdf

46. Sue, D., Sue, D. W., Sue, D., and Sue, S. (2022). *Understanding Abnormal Behavior (*12th Ed.). Cengage Learning.

47. Santiago, P. N., Ursano, R. J., Gray, C. L., Pynoos, R. S., Spiegel, S., Lewis-Fernandez, R., Friedman, M. J., and Fullerton, C. S. (2013). "A Systematic Review of PTSD Prevalence and Trajectories in DSM-5 Defined Trauma Exposed Populations: Intentional and Non-Intentional Traumatic Events." *PLOS One, 8*(4), e59236. https://doi.org/10.1371/journal.pone.0059236

48. Rothbaum, B., Foa, E., and Hembree, E. (2007). *Reclaiming Your Life from a Traumatic Experience: A Prolonged Exposure Treatment Program Workbook.* New York: Oxford University Press.

49. Resick, P. A., Monson, C. M., and Chard, K. M. (2014). "Cognitive Processing Therapy: Veteran/Military Version: Therapist and Patient Materials Manual." Washington, DC: Department of Veterans Affairs.

50. Lejuez, C. W., Hopko, D. R., and Hopko, S. D. (2001). "A Brief Behavioral Activation Treatment for Depression." *Behavior Modification, 25.* 255–286. [PubMed:11317637]

51. Dworkin, E. R. (2020). "Risk for Mental Disorders Associated with Sexual Assault: A Meta-analysis." *Trauma, Violence, & Abuse, 21*(5) 1011–1028. https://doi.org/10.1177/152438018813198

52. Bryant, R. A. (2013). "An Update of Acute Stress Disorder." *PTSD Research Quarterly, 24(1),* 1–7. https://www.ptsd.va.gov/publications/rq_docs/V24N1.pdf

53. Beck, A. T., Rush, A. K., Shaw, B. F., and Emery, G. (1979). *Cognitive Therapy of Depression.* New York: The Guilford Press.

54. Center for Substance Abuse Treatment, "Understanding the Impact of Trauma," "Trauma-Informed Care in Behavioral Health Services," NCBI Bookshelf, 2014, https://www.ncbi.nlm.nih.gov/books/NBK207191/.

55. Center for Substance Abuse Treatment, "Understanding the Impact of Trauma."

56. Regina Steil et al., "Dialectical Behavior Therapy for Posttraumatic Stress Disorder Related to Childhood Sexual Abuse: A Pilot Study of an Intensive Residential Treatment Program." *Journal of Traumatic Stress* 24, no. 1 (February 1, 2011): 102–106, https://doi.org/10.1002/jts.20617

57. Michele A. Schottenbauer et al., "Contributions of Psychodynamic Approaches to Treatment of PTSD and Trauma: A Review of the Empirical Treatment and Psychopathology Literature." *Psychiatry MMC* 71, no. 1 (March 1, 2008): 13–34, https://doi.org/10.1521/psyc.2008.71.1.13

58. Peter Payne, Peter Levine, and Mardi A. Crane-Godreau. "Somatic Experiencing: Using Interoception and Proprioception as Core Elements of Trauma Therapy." *Frontiers in Psychology* 6 (February 4, 2015), https://doi.org/10.3389/fpsyg.2015.00093

59. Russ Harris. "Embracing Your Demons: An Overview of Acceptance and Commitment Therapy." *Psychotherapy in Australia* 12, no. 4 (August 1, 2006): 70, https://search.informit.com.au/documentSummary;dn=545561433272993;res=IELHEA

60. Daphne M. Davis and Jeffrey A. Hayes. "What Are the Benefits of Mindfulness? A Practice Review of Psychotherapy-Related Research." *Psychotherapy* 48, no. 2 (January 1, 2011): 198–208, https://doi.org/10.1037/a0022062

61. Stefanie Malan-Müller et al., "The Gut Microbiome and Mental Health: Implications for Anxiety- and Trauma-Related Disorders." *OMICS: a Journal of Integrative Biology* 22, no. 2 (February 1, 2018): 90–107, https://doi.org/10.1089/omi.2017.0077

62. Greenwald, R. (2013). *Progressive Counting within a Phase Model of Trauma-Informed Treatment*. New York: Routledge.

63. Sable, P. (1995). "Pets, Attachment, and Well-Being across the Life Cycle." *Social Work,* 40, 334–341.

64. Va.gov: *Veterans Affairs. Dogs and PTSD* (2012, December 31). Retrieved April 5, 2023, from https://www.ptsd.va.gov/gethelp/dogs_ptsd.asp

65. Greenwald, R. (2007). *EMDR within a Phase Model of Trauma-Informed Treatment*. New York: Haworth.

66. Stacey M. Schaefer et al., "Purpose in Life Predicts Better Emotional Recovery from Negative Stimuli." *PLOS ONE* 8, no. 11 (November 13, 2013): e80329, https://doi.org/10.1371/journal.pone.0080329

Index

abuser
  living with, 30–31
  seeing in court, 180–81
  survivors on knowing their, 15–17
acceptance and commitment therapy (ACT), 230–31
acquaintance rape. *See* date rape
active coping strategy, 82–84
active listening, 32, 36
acts of kindness, 121–22
acupuncturists, 111–12
acute stress disorder (ASD), 224–25, 226
addiction counseling, 231
adrenaline, 228
adverse childhood experiences (ACEs), 228
advocates. *See also* sexual violence advocates; victim advocates
  being an ally, 255–57
  continuing support after sexual violence, 32–33
  role of, 27–29
affirmations, 84, 135, 232–35
agoraphobia, 224, *225,* 226
alcohol-facilitated sexual assault, 8–9, 20, 172, 183
alcohol use disorder, 221, 224, *225,* 227, 228
allies (allyship), 255–57
altruism, 249–53
American Bar Association Criminal Justice Standards for Prosecution Function, 161–62
anger, 77, 83, 105, 159
  after criminal trial verdict, 206–7

animal therapy, 30, 238–39, 272–74
anxiety, 9, 86, 218–19, 224, *225,* 227, 262
  children and, 12
  during criminal trials, 149, 167, 177, 180, 183, 185, 202
  defense mechanisms, 77, 78
  managing during investigation, 150, 154, 157–58
  nutrition and, 236
Archambault, Joanne, 170
arousal, 8, 219
  myth about erection or orgasm, 19–20
art therapy, 231
avoidance, 77, 115, 224, 226, 227
Ayana Therapists, 34
azithromycin, 53

bailiffs, 175, 203
bathing
  DNA evidence and avoiding, 44, 51–52, 54
  self-care, 47, 85
Bathory, Patricia, 22–23, 82–84, 205–7
behavioral activation (BA), 225
bench trials, 166, 202
"beyond a reasonable doubt," 162, 202–4
bipolar disorders, 224, *225,* 226
Black Emotional and Mental Health Collective, 35
Black women, 33–36
Black Women's Blueprint, 35
Black Women's Health Imperative, 35
blame. *See* self-blame; victim blaming
Boardman, Justin, 8–9, 150–55

About the Author

Cheyenne Wilson, BSN, founder of We Are the Evidence, is on a mission to raise awareness about the reality of sexual assault, eliminate the stigma associated with being a victim of this violent crime, and make lasting changes in the justice and health care systems. Cheyenne earned her bachelor's in psychology and worked in social services before pursuing a career in nursing.